...k Slouka earned his Ph.D. from Columbia University, ...re he also gained his M.Phil., M.A. and B.A. cum ... ...e. He has worked as a Teaching Fellow at Harvard, ...s currently a Lecturer at the University of California ...n ...n Diego.

War of the Worlds

CYBERSPACE AND THE HIGH-TECH ASSAULT ON REALITY

Mark Slouka

An *Abacus* Book

First published in the United States of America by
Basic Books 1995
First published in Great Britain by
Abacus 1996
Reprinted 1996

A CIP catalogue record for this book
is available from the British Library

Typeset by Palimpsest Book Productions Limited,
Polmont, Stirlingshire
Printed and bound in Great Britain by
Clays Ltd, St Ives plc

UK companies, institutions and other organisations wishing
to make bulk purchases of this or any other book
published by Little, Brown should contact their local
bookshop or the special sales department at the address below.
Tel 0171 911 8000. Fax 0171 911 8100.

Abacus
A Division of
Little, Brown and Company (UK)
Brettenham House
Lancaster Place
London WC2E 7EN

For Leslie, Zack, and Maya,
my one reality

Everything informational and important to the life of individuals . . . will be found for sale, or for the taking, in cyberspace.

– Michael Benedikt, *Cyberspace: First Steps*

Contents

Acknowledgments

This is a personal book; it follows that my debts to those who helped me with and through it would be largely personal as well. For most, in fact, the word *debt* seems too harsh. I thank them – a small and special circle – for their help, their generosity, their friendship. They can expect as much of me in turn.

Though it seems customary in proceedings of this sort to save mention of immediate family members for last, my case requires a new order. Whatever is good and right about this book is due in no small part to my wife, Leslie Gollin Slouka, whose heart and mind I have relied on, in this as in most things, the way a carpenter relies on his level. Many of the ideas found here were originally hers; many others, the products of our days together. In a very real sense, this work was a collaboration, and the only reason her name doesn't appear next to mine is because she didn't wish it to.

As to the rest, I owe thanks to Andy Mannle, who read large parts of the early manuscript; Joseph Nirdlinger, who gave unstintingly of his time and energy and listened to my theories with patience and goodwill; and Larry Sawh, who lighted the way into cyberspace. I am grateful as well to Wendy Graham and Jennifer Jestin for their critical readings of the manuscript in its later stages. At Basic Books, my editor, Susan Rabiner, was a great help in giving this project shape while leaving its particular spirit intact, while Linda Carbone performed small miracles in moving the manuscript through the later stages. My agents, Arnold and Elise Goodman, were particularly helpful not only in finding this book a home but in saving its author from more than his share of pitfalls. To the small circle of my colleagues and friends at Eleanor Roosevelt College at the University of California, San Diego – Nicole Tonkovich, Rebecca Arnold, Mollie Martinek, and Erin Klein – I owe thanks for encouragement as well as, at times, for covering my back.

Others, among them Joanne Isaac and Beth Beringer, I can thank only for their patience with me during a time when I was mentally more often absent than not (I hope they'll notice the difference). Finally, to Sydney Lea (who understands the value of place better than anyone I know), I am grateful as one is grateful to another who confirms his beliefs and, occasionally, corrects his course.

On another level, of course, I owe a debt to all those, from Thomas Carlyle to Daniel Boorstin, who helped blaze the trail I walk in this book. Among contemporaries I'm particularly grateful to Bill McKibben, Sven Birkerts, and Neil Postman. Not only did their works provide pleasure and inspiration along the way but their spirit confirmed my belief that the best critiques are often, as Camus told us, the most passionate affirmations as well.

To my parents, finally, I am grateful for teaching me long ago that here, on *this* Earth, in *this* time, among the lives we've each come to know – and not on some virtual plane –

is where we find both our greatest pleasure and our deepest responsibility. Without my parents, my allegiances would be of a different sort, I would be a different man, and this would be a very different book.

Introduction

The Road to Unreality

In 1990, a reporter for the *New York Times*, following the famous case of a man accused of murdering his pregnant wife and then blaming the assault on an unknown black assailant, asked a neighbor of the couple for her thoughts on the tragedy. Do you accept his story? she was asked. Does it seem possible to you, knowing this man, that he made up the whole thing? 'I don't know,' the woman replied, 'I'm dying for the movie to come out so I can see how it ends.'[1]

I don't think this woman was joking. Or being cynical. Or even evasive. I think she simply meant what she said. For her, a TV movie about the tragedy would tell her – more accurately than her own experience – what to believe. It would settle for her what was real. Less than a year later, the made-for-television movie 'Good Night, Sweet Wife: A Murder in Boston' presumably did just that.

I bring up this episode for the light it sheds on an important cultural trend, a trend so pervasive as to be almost invisible: our growing separation from reality.[2] More and more of us, whether we realize it or not, accept the copy as the original. Increasingly removed from experience, overdependent on the representations of reality that come to us through television and the print media, we seem more and more willing to put our trust in intermediaries who 're-present' the world to us.

The problem with this is one of communication; intermediaries are notoriously unreliable. In the well-known children's game of telephone, a whispered message is passed along from person to person until it is garbled beyond recognition. If we think of that original message as truth, or reality, we stand today at the end of a long line of interpreters. It's a line that's been growing longer throughout the century. And now, accustomed to our place at the end of that line, we've begun to accept the fictions that reach us as the genuine article. This is not good news. For one thing, it threatens to make us stupid. For another, it makes us, collectively, gullible as children: we believe what we are told. Finally, it can make us dangerous.

When did we start accepting abstractions for the real thing? Most answers point roughly to the beginning of this century. Before 1900, daily life for the majority of individuals was agrarian, static, local – in other words, not that different from what it had been for centuries. The twentieth century, however, altered the pace and pattern of daily life forever. Within two generations, the old world (for better and worse) was gone. Its loss meant the loss of two things that had always grounded us: our place within an actual community and our connection to a particular physical landscape.[3]

What started us on the road to unreality? Though the catalog reads like a shopping list of many of the century's most dramatic trends – urbanization, consumerism, increasing mobility, loss of regionality, growing alienation from the landscape, and so on – technology, their common denominator, was the real force behind our journey toward abstraction.

A single example may make my point. As everyone knows, unreality increases with speed. Walking across a landscape at six miles an hour, we experience the particular reality of place: its smells, sounds, colors, textures, and so on. Driving at seventy miles an hour, the experience is very different. The car isolates us, distances us; the world beyond the windshield – whether desert mesa or rolling farmland – seems vaguely unreal. At supersonic speeds, the divorce is complete. A landscape at 30,000 feet is an abstraction, as unlike real life as a painting.

It's an unreality we've grown used to. Habit has dulled the strangeness of it. We're as comfortable with super-human speed – and the level of abstraction it brings with it – as we are with, say, the telephone, which in a single stroke distanced us from a habit as old as our species: talking to one another face-to-face. We forget that initial users of the telephone (our grandmothers and grandfathers) found it nearly impossible to conceptualize another human being beyond the inanimate receiver; in order to communicate, they had to personify the receiver and speak *to* it, as to some mechanical pet, rather than *through* it to someone else. Today, that kind of instinctive attachment to physical reality seems quaint.

We've come a long way, very quickly. What surprises us now, increasingly, is the shock of the real: the nakedness of face-to-face communication, the rough force of the natural world. We can watch hours of nature programming, but place us in a forest or a meadow and we don't know quite what to do with ourselves. We look forward to hanging out at The Brick with Chris on *Northern Exposure* but dread running into our neighbor while putting out the trash. There has come to be something almost embarrassing about the unmediated event; the man or woman who takes out a musical instrument at a party and offers to play is likely to make everyone feel a bit awkward. It's so naked, somehow. We're more comfortable with its representation: Aerosmith on MTV, Isaac Stern or Eric Clapton on CD.

And now, as we close out the century, various computer technologies threaten to take our long journey from reality to its natural conclusion. They are to TV or videoconferencing what the Concorde is to the car. They have the capacity to make the partially synthetic environments we already inhabit complete – to remove us, once and for all, from reality.

Let me state my case as directly as possible: I believe it is possible to see, in a number of technologies spawned by recent developments in the computer world, an attack on reality as human beings have always known it. I believe this process has been under way for some time, that it will be aided immeasurably by the so-called digital revolution currently sweeping through the industrialized world, and that its implications for our culture are enormous.

I'm the first to admit that this may seem an absurd contention. Most of us, after all, have little trouble separating reality from illusion. We know, for example, that Homer Simpson is a cartoon character on TV, while our neighbor, however much he may act like one, is not; that the highway during our morning commute, the sky at noon, or the bird on the wire at dusk, are not hallucinations; that a drawing of a two-by-four does not a two-by-four make.

Within a few years, however, distinctions such as these will be less automatic. We'll be able to pick up an electronically generated two-by-four. Feel its weight. Swing it around. Whack somebody with it. And yet none of it – not the two-by-four, the person we hit, or the landscape in

4

which this takes place – will be real, in the usual, physical sense. We'll be able to immerse ourselves in an entirely synthetic world, a world that exists only as a trick of the senses, a computer-induced hallucination. And when we emerge from cyberspace – that strange nonplace beyond the computer screen – all indicators suggest that we will find it increasingly difficult to separate real life (already demoted to the acronym RL on computer Nets around the world) from virtual existence. Or worse, that we will know the difference but opt for the digitized world over the real one.

However futuristic all this may sound, it's not all that new. In May 1938, in an essay written for *Harper's Magazine*, E.B. White predicted the encroachment of technology on what we might call the territory of the real. 'Clearly,' he noted, 'the race today is . . . between the things that are and the things that seem to be, between the chemist at RCA and the angel of God.' Already, he pointed out, sound effects had begun taking the place of sound itself. Television and radio were enlarging the eye's range, advertising an abstract place, an Elsewhere, that would grow to seem increasingly real. In time, he concluded, *representations* of life, seen on radio and television and in the movies, would come to seem more lifelike to us than their originals.[4]

White called it perfectly. Only months after his prediction, citizens up and down the Eastern seaboard of the United States were heading for the hills, panicked by Orson Welles's radio adaptation of H. G. Wells's *War of the Worlds* into believing that sixteen-tentacled Martians had landed on Earth. It was a dramatic victory for the chemist at RCA and a defining moment for the New Age. For the thousands who rushed north to escape the Martians' onslaught, Welles's electronic illusion easily triumphed over common sense *and* reality.

The Martians (or the forces of electronic illusion) have been rolling on ever since. The war of the worlds – pitting physical reality against the forces of Elsewhere – continues, and reality continues to take it on the chin. In Yugoslavia recently, an actor who had portrayed the deceased dictator Marshal Tito in a docudrama found himself applauded, and reviled, by ordinary citizens on the streets of Belgrade. In Rio de Janeiro, when a soap opera villain murdered his co-star in real life, the actual homicide and the tortured plot of the *telenovela* fused seamlessly in the public mind. When the National Weather Service interrupted daytime programming to issue a tornado warning for a county in Kansas, the local TV station was flooded with phone calls from outraged citizens incensed over having to miss their soaps.[5]

But television's transgressions on the territory of the real are just minor skirmishes compared to the all-out assault being conducted by the digital avant-garde. The race, you see, is no longer between the angel of God and the chemist at RCA. It's between the angel of God and the computer visionary at Microsoft. Or Apple. Or MIT. And he's not interested in imitating reality; he's out to replace it altogether. What the computer world is doing, says John Perry Barlow, Grateful Dead lyricist-turned-computer-cowboy, 'is taking material and making it immaterial: Now is the flesh made word, in many respects.'[6]

Reduced to its essentials, it comes down to this: only a decade after White's death, we stand on the threshold of turning life itself into computer code, of transforming the experience of living in the physical world – every sensation, every detail – into a product for our consumption. 'We now have the ability,' says Barlow, 'to take the sum of human experience and give it a medium in which to flow.' What this means, simply, is that computer simulations may soon be so pervasive (and so realistic) that life itself will require some sort of mark of authenticity. Reality, in other words, may one day come with an asterisk.[7]

None of which should come as much of a surprise. These, after all, are the days of miracle and wonder, of 'telepresence' and 'immersion technology' (which promise to submerge us in a fully sensual, synthetic world), of intelligent software, artificial life, and virtual damn-near everything. Entire virtual communities, some numbering ten thousand citizens and more, are now accessible through the conceptual window of your computer screen. Many have homes, prostitutes, tree houses for your children. Within five years, according to John Quarterman, a cyberspace cartographer, the digital world will be inhabited by over a billion individuals worldwide. Those of us still on the outside, Professor Timothy Ferris of Berkeley informs us, will be able to 'watch grandmothers be shot by snipers in Sarajevo from six camera angles' without leaving our couches.[8]

Even for the technologically literate, it can all seem vaguely surreal, a strange mixture of hard science and science fiction, binary code and bubble gum. Our home computers, to take just one example, will soon come with a face capable of responding to our expressions, understanding our gestures, even reading our lips. Its eyes will follow us around the room. We'll be able to talk with it, argue with it, flirt with it. We'll be able to program it to look like our husband or our child. Or the Holy See, I suppose. Will it have emotions? You bet. Scream at it and it will cower, or cringe. Maybe even cry. 'What we want is not intelligence,' says Akikazu Takeuchi, a researcher at the Sony Computer Science Laboratory, 'but humanity.'[9]

What are we to make of this large-scale tinkering with

the human mind and its time-tested orbit? What should those of us in RL make of the dizzying proliferation (and ever-increasing sophistication) of cyberspace communities – the so-called MUDs and MOOs and MUSHes? Or of the fact that an entire generation of *computerjugen*[10] is now spending its leisure time in electronically generated space, experiencing what cyberspace theorists like to call 'lucid dreaming in an awake state'?[11] Or that cyberization – the movement to animate everyday objects in order to make them more responsive to our needs – is making rapid progress? In a word, how seriously should we be taking all this?

I'd like to suggest that we take it *very* seriously. Why? Because technology is never a neutral force: it orders our behavior, redefines our values, reconstitutes our lives in ways we can't always predict. Like a political constitution or a legislative act, as Langdon Winner, professor of political science at Rensselaer Polytechnic Institute, has noted, technology establishes the rules by which people live.[12] The digital revolution is technology with a capital T. And its rules, I suspect, may not be to everyone's liking.

Given the enormous effect the digital revolution may come to have on our lives (the digerati, as Steve Lohr has called them,[13] routinely liken its impact to that of the splitting of the atom, the invention of the Gutenberg Press, and the discovery of fire), there is something downright eerie about the lack of debate, the conspicuous absence of dissenting voices, the silence of the critics. Congress seems uninterested; watchdog groups sleep. Like shined deer, we seem to be wandering en masse onto the digital highway, and the only concern heard in the land, by and large, is that some of us may be left behind.[14] Under the circumstances, some caution is surely in order, particularly if we consider that the digital revolution is having its greatest effect on the young. Think of this book as a speed bump on the fiber-optic highway.

My gripe, I should point out, is not so much with the technologies themselves as with the general lack of concern over the consequences that many new applications may come to have. I'm a humanist, not a Luddite. Though I'll admit to a certain fondness for old-fashioned pastimes (I'll take a book or a musical instrument over a Mac and a modem), I'm not incapable of appreciating the contemporary wonders – from gene splicing to lasers – that everywhere crowd in on our attention. I'm not insensitive to the benefits and beauties of technology; without them, my wife and my son would have died during childbirth.

So let me be as clear as possible: I have no problem with what Andrew S. Grove, president and CEO of the Intel Corporation, has called 'the ubiquitous PC.'[15] I own and use one. Nor do I have any argument, for example, with the millions of people who crowd the 'chat groups' available on the Net (many of whom I've found to be no more or less decent and interesting than people in the real world). My quarrel is with a relatively small but disproportionately influential group of self-described 'Net religionists' and 'wannabe gods' who believe that the physical world can (and should) be 'downloaded' into a computer, who believe that the future of mankind is not in RL (real life) but in some form of VR (virtual reality); who are working very hard (and spending enormous amounts of both federal and private money) to engineer their very own version of the apocalypse. As intelligent as they are single-minded, these people have been ignored by the majority of humanists for too long; it's time we started listening.

The *real* issue here, as the novelist and technoevangelist Robert Coover has pointed out, is how we answer the question, 'What's human?' For some, he explains, humanity 'has to do with souls and "depth" and the search for meaning and purpose; with tradition, ritual, mystery and individualism.' For others, like himself, it has more to do with the spiritualism of the hive: the increasingly inter-linked system of computers and computer technologies about to subsume (as Kevin Kelly, the executive editor of *Wired* magazine, recently put it) the 'millions of buzzing, dim-witted personal computers' (that's us) into one grand organism/machine immeasurably greater than the sum of its parts. For Coover (as for others, including Speaker of the House of Representatives Newt Gingrich), our 'evolution' into this hive state is inevitable. 'I regret,' he says, 'having to give up the comforting fairy tales of the past: I, too, want to be unique, significant, connected to a "deeper truth," canonized. I want to *have* an "I." Too bad.'[16]

Of course, shedding 'fairy tales' like tradition, individu-alism, and identity, Coover admits, may have its downside. 'If creatures of the past were hived under queen bees like Alexander the Great or Genghis Khan,' he points out (quite reasonably, I think), 'it seems unlikely that hived creatures of the future will escape their own hive-masters.' And what, one might wonder, will happen to the 'unhived'? 'No doubt they will get stepped on,' says Coover; 'the Sophist principle "knowledge is power" will make them mere meat at the fringe.'

The expression 'meat at the fringe,' I think, comes close to explaining what this book is about. When a significant number of powerful individuals – scientists, academics, authors, engineers, computer programmers – following the scent of a potential $3.5 *trillion* industry[17] begin referring to the human body as meat (the expression is a common one among the digerati), it's time for those still foolishly attached to theirs to start paying attention. When a subculture of enthusiasts yearning for the technological equivalent of rapture begins labeling the unhived (in a weak attempt at digital wit) PONAs (people of no account), the PONAs may want to start asking what counts and what doesn't.

'When the yearning for human flesh has come to an end,' asks Barlow, referring to the human touch, not to cannibalism, 'what will remain?' Good question. 'Mind,' he says hopefully, 'may continue, uploaded into the Net, suspended in an ecology of voltage as ambitiously capable of self-sustenance as was that of its carbon-based forebears.'[18] To unhived PONAs like myself, this is hardly encouraging. I *like* my carbon-based body and the carbon-based bodies of my wife and children and friends. I like my carbon-based dog and my carbon-based garden. Nor, to pick up on Coover's 'meat on the fringe' image, do I particularly fancy myself as roadkill on the digital highway.

My uneasiness with the new transcendentalists, I suppose, springs from my own instinctive allegiance to the physical world, to the present moment, to the strengths and limitations of the human mind. I'm suspicious of whatever tends to improve or displace these. I believe we all should be. I believe that tampering with the primary things in life (our sense of reality, for example, or individual identity) is not to be undertaken lightly, that technological progress sometimes is and sometimes ain't, and that the cloak of inevitability (the technologists' time-tested method for steamrolling dissent or even debate) has been known to conceal both miracles and monsters.

Coover and Co. may find my timidity quaint, my values hopelessly sentimental. I can live with that. What it comes down to, it seems to me, is this: human culture depends on the shared evidence of the senses, always has; we can communicate with one another because a hurled rock will always break skin, a soap bubble always burst. A technology designed to short-circuit the senses, a technology capable of providing an alternate world – abstract, yet fully inhabitable, real to our senses yet accessible only through a computer screen – would take away this common ground and replace it with one manufactured for us by the technologists.

And this is not a good thing. Why? Because human history, in the largest sense, has been the record of our debate with the world. Because reality has been and continues to be the great touchstone for the world's ethical systems. Because, simply put, the world provides context, and without context, ethical behavior is impossible. It is the physical facts of birth and pain and pleasure and death that force us (enable us) to make value judgments: *this* is better than *that*. Nourishment is better than hunger. Compassion is better than torture. Virtual systems, by offering us a reality divorced from the world, from the limits and responsibilities of presence, offer us as well a glimpse into an utterly amoral universe. Consider an obvious example: in Night Trap, a CD-Rom video game recently popular among prepubescent boys, vampires drill holes into the necks of their barely clad female victims and hang them from meat hooks; virtual reality (coming soon to a modem near you) will allow you to *be* the vampire. To inflict pain. Without responsibility. Without consequences. The punctured flesh will heal at the touch of a button, the scream disappear into cyberspace. You'll be able to resurrect the digital dead and kill them again.

The implications of these new technologies are social; the questions they pose, broadly ethical; the risks they entail, unprecedented. They are the cultural equivalent of genetic engineering, except that in this experiment, even more than in the other one, *we* will be the potential new hybrids, the two-pound mice.

What will technologies that alter our sense of reality mean, in the long run? What will they do to us? No one knows. Ask the technovisionaries how human beings (who have evolved over millions of years in response to the constraints and pressures of the physical world) might respond to existence in aphysical environments, or to the wholesale cyberization of the human environment, and they'll fall over one another in their willingness to admit that they have no idea. Does this concern them just a little? Frighten them, maybe? Not a bit. 'The best things in life are scary,' Kevin Kelly told me recently, 'I'm serious.'[19] Unfortunately for the rest of us, he probably is. So on we go, blindfolded, pedal to the floor, over the canyonlands.

Does my concern spring from a lack of vision? Apparently not. Not long ago, I asked John Perry Barlow what the advantages might be to leaving the physical world behind. 'Damned few,' he wrote back, 'for any individual as presently configured. But advantage,' he went on, 'has nothing to do with it. There are many evolutionary forces at work here, most of them working against us. All of them inexorable.' But what about all that business of leaving the flesh behind, I asked, of uploading ourselves into the Net? 'Again,' he answered, 'it's less a matter of advantage than inevitability. It's happening and will continue to. If I could stop it I would.' But what, I asked, would you say to those who might be terrified by this prospect (of transcending the meat, so to speak)? 'They're right,' said Barlow, wrapping up with a philosophical shrug. 'But when you're about to be swept over the falls, you might as well try to enjoy the ride.'[20]

I am no Oliver Stone. I have no interest in conspiracy

theories. Nor do I wish to gloss over the very real benefits the digital New Age may bring; technology, as I have said, is never a wholly one-sided affair. My concern, rather, is based on a small number of well-worn truths: that the free market can unleash forces difficult to control; that technological innovation has its own logic, often separate from questions of value and ethics; and that *some* technologies – particularly those that promise (or threaten) to transform human culture as we know it – bear watching.

CHAPTER I

'Reality Is Death'
THE SPIRIT OF CYBERSPACE

I first stumbled upon (or into) the world of virtual systems while teaching undergraduate seminars on twentieth-century culture at a major California university. The head lecturer, an intelligent and witty woman, was, it turned out, an expert on cyberspace, or the closest thing to an expert possible in an area of study still essentially in its embryonic state, dominated by hackers from a half-dozen related fields.

Every course has its own signature. In the stresses and gaps, we can read the lecturer's own interests. The first thing that struck me about this particular class (a ten-week survey of contemporary culture from World War I to the present 'and beyond') was the unusual emphasis on Nietzsche and the Dadaists. Students largely innocent of the Triple Alliance and the Munich Pact, the decline of European economic hegemony and the effects of decolonization, could explain the significance of automatic writing, identify and discuss Duchamp's Fountain, recite Nietzsche's dictum 'the breaker is the creator.' Virtually all understood the validity of the attack on rationalism and objectivity, the moral bankruptcy of Western liberalism.

None of which, of course, was particularly new or disturbing. Clearly, the well-worn theme, so suited to adolescents ripe for reductive conspiracy theories, was the imperialism of 'value structures' as such. Objectivity was a lie. History was a lie. Truth, as the anarchist Mikhail Bakunin had noted, was nothing more than a stick with which the mighty beat the weak. I'd heard it before. I was reasonably comfortable with it. A good deal of it I even agreed with. When the brush strokes got a little broad, I'd use my weekly discussion sections to qualify, elaborate. Every week I'd patiently, stubbornly reintroduce the problem of ethics into the equation of modern culture.

And yet, over time, it became progressively more difficult to ignore the discomfort I felt. To students, I could paper over any obvious differences between the lecturer and myself by referring to the dialectical nature of academic discourse. I had a harder time convincing myself. I liked this person. I liked talking to her. We were both on the Left. We had a similar sense of humor. Why was it, then, that I found myself – internally, subtly – more and more antagonistic toward her?

It wasn't until the last lecture that the seemingly random points of discomfort coalesced into an image I could understand. The subject was the future. I expected something on the post-cold war balance of power, the rise of tribalism, the revolutionary implications – for notions of state sovereignty, for example – of environmental degradation. The subject, instead, was the role virtual technologies would play in the new century.

Already, we were told, technological prostheses had begun to 'liberate' us from the limitations of the human body. The possibilities were endless. Within the span of our children's lifetimes, we were assured, it would be possible to link the human nervous system directly to a computer, to download the human consciousness into RAM (random access memory), effectively preserving it in some artificial state. Within the foreseeable future, the dividing line between nature and technology – a false dichotomy, we were told, since at least the invention of agriculture – would be erased; genetic engineering in general, and the Human Genome Project in particular, had already blurred the line forever.

Cyberspace systems would develop and expand, fundamentally altering our definitions of physical space, of identity and community. Already it was routinely possible to interface simultaneously with a number of different individuals in different parts of the globe. In the not-too-distant future, it would be possible to touch them. Feedback technology would provide the illusion of touch directly to your nervous system. It would be indistinguishable from the real thing. Physical presence would become optional; in time, an affectation. And, having marginalized the physical self, we would marginalize community (in the old sense of the word) as well; a new era in human evolution would be ushered in. Divorced from our bodies, our minds grafted onto computers capable of realizing for us the contents of our imagination (or allowing us to experience another's imagination), meeting one another in electronically generated spaces with their own rules of behavior, we would finally attain the fulfillment of our species. In this New Age, boundaries between self and other, male and female, nature and machine, even life and death, would be obsolete. The word *reality* would lose all meaning, or would metastasize beyond recognition. Death, truly, would have no dominion. If you missed your wife or husband, whose physical body had died, you could meet up again in the virtual world. Take a walk together. Drink cappuccino. Have sex.

There was more. It was quite a lecture. My first response, I'll confess, was one of amusement. It seemed ripe territory for a new genre of jokes. Would all this spawn a new generation of travel agents? Virtual vacations? If someone told you to fuck yourself, could you do it?

Amusement gradually shifted to mild fascination. All this talk of immortality, of an 'other' world; all this hostility toward the body – what was it but a rather unoriginal techno-Christianity? Substitute a few terms, look beneath the technological jargon, and you had the same basic structures, the same motivations and fears. As an example of the adaptability of a cultural form, it was moderately interesting, nothing more. The prophecies themselves seemed absurd, silly, an adolescent fantasy.

Why, then, if the material was so transparent, so easily dismissed, did my curiosity give way to irritation? Why, during the week following that last lecture, did I keep picking at it, arguing with it? Why, finally, did I find it so disturbing when I brought my three-year-old son with me to pick up the final exams, to see the lecturer hand him a two-inch hybrid animal, half elephant, half cow? She had an entire collection of the little monstrosities in her office. Rabbits with pigs' snouts. Galloping horses with big dogs' heads. My son, who will play with damn near anything, wouldn't touch them. 'I didn't like those funny animals,' he told me on the way back to the car.

I didn't either. It was the process of trying to figure out *why* I didn't like them that first suggested to me the significance of the instinctive resistance I'd been feeling those past ten weeks. What I had been reacting to, I realized, was a kind of technological absolutism, a willingness to tinker with (or disregard) the lives of mere men and women for the sake of some future ideal. Totalists of all stripes, after all, have always been linked by their common desire to transform the world in their own image. Totalitarian visions – whether utopian fantasies or dystopian nightmares – have shared an aversion to the world in all its quotidian messiness, as well as a corresponding preoccupation with cleanliness, order, control. All, similarly, have been characterized by a vast arrogance, an unshakable belief in their own vision of a different world.

But totalitarianism destroyed one *part* of the world for the sake of another. Theorists in virtual systems, if anything, went further; their disdain for the world was more complete. They weren't interested in regaining some nationalized vision of rural bliss, some Teutonic or pan-Slavic *heimat*; they wanted the apocalypse. Their sensibility, in other words (though the distinction is a precarious one), seemed less political than religious.

But even religious absolutism fell short. Christianity, for example, unparalleled in its ability to deny the world and denounce the body, to subordinate this life to the next, nonetheless drew the majority of its forms from *this* world, from existing structures: the *rock* of the church; the *tree* of life; the *community* of Christ. And these, it had always seemed to me, suggested a latent nostalgia. Beneath the hate for this fallen Earth, beneath the blood of the Book of Revelation, lurked a suppressed yearning. The New Jerusalem, after all, would descend to us, to *this* Earth. The cyberspace revolution, by contrast, would seek to erase the world as we had known it. It was of the same spirit as Christianity, but bigger. Colder. And melodramatic as it may seem, I sensed in it a fundamental threat to life as I'd always conceived it, as existence *within* the world. It was our connection to the physical world, I'd always believed – however ephemeral, however fragile – that gave strength, courage, even love, their meaning. But these concerns, in the world of cyberspace, were already anachronistic. What was strength, or courage, in a world without risk? What was love if not a voluntary loss of control? What was love, after all, without mortality?

What I had been confronting, in short, was an ethical vacuum. What I had sensed was an utter lack of compassion for the world and its problems as they are. Why speak of the destruction of real communities in the Balkans when you can inhabit virtual ones? Why bring up the importance of biodiversity and the implications of habitat destruction when you can create your *own* environment? From the lecturer's point of view, nature already *was* technology; in her future, the hybrid – symbolic of the newly blurred boundaries between the sexes, between species, between entire kingdoms – would be the new incarnation. It seemed to me then (and I am not naturally given to apocalyptic imagery) that the beast slouching towards Bethlehem would be a child with the head of a dog, and the sand itself, the burning heat, a desert in cyberspace, a virtual dream.

It was at this point, I think, that I began noticing the frequency with which the *cyber-* and *hyper-* prefixes appeared in the mass media, the extent to which the new technology had percolated downward through the system. At my neighborhood newsstand (always a telling barometer of cultural trends), my attention was caught by the premier issue of *Future Sex* magazine, which, besides promising to fill me in on the New World Order in adult video and answer all my questions regarding electronic masturbation, claimed to have the latest word on cyborg sex slaves, 3D digital orgasms, and virtual reality sex.

The latest word, it turned out, was that in the near future, we would be able to have sex in virtual space.

The computer would make our fantasies real. Cyborgs, created to our specifications, electronically generated but palpable to our senses, would form a new generation of slaves. We would be their creators. The possibilities of hyperfucking, the editors assured me, would have no impact on real-world relationships. I could hardly wait. The accompanying illustration showed a tangerine-colored 'woman,' with large breasts and a prehensile tail, having sex with a sort of plum-colored devil. She had two heads, neither of which looked particularly happy.[1]

When a new technology has been appropriated by science fiction freaks and popularizers, as well as given recognition by the arbiters of high culture (one shelf down from *Future Sex*, the term *hyperworld* called out from the cover of *The New Yorker*), we can assume it has caught the attention of a mass audience. I decided to look further into the whole business of cyberspace research.

What I discovered fairly quickly was that virtual systems (articles on cyborg love slaves aside) had an unusually impressive genealogy. Cyberspace research, I found, was originally underwritten in the late 1980s by a consortium of military interests – primarily the Defense Advanced Research Products Agency, or DARPA – hoping to develop a virtual environment for large-scale military exercises. Faced with the escalating costs, both financial and political, of conducting war games in Western Europe, the Pentagon decided to develop a virtual battlefield. They threw open the R&D coffers, began the bidding, and soon the thing was done. The SIMNET system linked 200 M1 tanks, each carrying a crew of four, moving over a computer-generated terrain visible through the tanks' ports. Vehicles and even aircraft would be visible to the crew; they could hear enemy as well as friendly fire. It was the beginning of a beautiful friendship between researchers in virtual systems and the bottomless pockets of the military that has continued to the present day.

The Defense Department was just one of many suitors. Reading the list, I began to understand the momentum that the new technology had acquired. From its beginnings in Air Force laboratories and the Draper Lab at the Massachusetts Institute of Technology, cyberspace research had attracted the funds and research facilities of university programs, such as those at the University of North Carolina and the Human Interface Technology Lab at the University of Washington; of computer giants like Atari, Apple, and Sega; of communications monoliths like AT&T; of multinational conglomerates like Warner Communications and Matsushita (which owns Panasonic and Universal), as well as any number of smaller companies scattered all over the industrialized world. The applications of the technology turned out to be as multifaceted as the technology itself was protean: this, in turn, led to an exceptionally fluid relationship between the public and private sectors. A video-equipped helmet, for example, though developed primarily at NASA's Ames Research Laboratories, quickly attracted the attention of companies interested in adapting it to TV, video games, advertising, and film.[2]

At this point, one thing began to seem fairly obvious: virtual systems were not a fad. They were not going to go away. Some applications had entered the market already; others massed on the borders. At the Flower Hill Mall near my home, I could put on a special helmet equipped with small video monitors capable of manufacturing a stereoscopic image before my eyes and maneuver through a stable, three-dimensional world generated entirely by a computer. If I turned my head, the computer would track my movements and adjust the view accordingly. By adding special stereo headphones, I could make that virtual world acoustically as well as visually complete. Ten minutes of virtual reality for five bucks.

Soon, the young man who set me up assured me, I'd be able to wear special gloves, and even a bodysuit, wired with position and motion transmitters that would represent my movements (to myself as well as to others) in the virtual world. Within a few years, that glove or bodysuit would be able to telegraph back to me the presence of virtual solid objects: their weight, texture, even temperature. I'd be able to immerse myself in a completely artificial world, in what those in the field were referring to as 'a fully englobing environment.'[3]

Was this a good thing? Did we *need* a fully englobing environment? I'd periodically pose this question to the various enthusiasts I encountered in both the real and the virtual world. Almost invariably, the question would strike them as odd, even absurd, the product of a distinctly nineteenth-century sensibility. Almost without exception, they'd answer not, as I expected, with an a priori yes but, rather, with a confused shrug. They didn't understand the question. How did I mean, *good?* The implicit motto seemed to be: we tinker because we can; if we weren't meant to blur the boundaries between self and other, nature and technology, solitude and community, they wouldn't allow themselves to be tampered with. They would resist us. It was precisely this untroubled, childlike, essentially pre-ethical attitude that I found most unsettling. Children, I thought, also see resistance as some sort of moral boundary, and will tear the wings off flies because they can – until someone suggests that they stop.

I pressed on, like some latter-day Alice, further behind the looking glass, hoping to find something that would help me understand the phenomenon of virtual systems, that would explain their appeal. In the borderless, timeless world I'd found myself in, there were no givens, no facts, no a priori truths. Individual identity, physical space, reality itself, had turned plastic and malleable, mere constructs we might choose to buy into, or reinterpret, or discard altogether – as we saw fit. Which of the three options we chose didn't matter. My lecturer, I began to realize, had a lot of company. Her views, far from representing the radical fringe as I had assumed, were representative of the cyberspace community as a whole. 'There's nothing "real" out there,' I was told on the Net by one resident of a cyberspace community. 'Reality is just a habit. A way of thinking. It's all just information.' When I asked whether he was being serious, he told me he wasn't interested in debating the obvious, and suggested I do some reading. 'Read a fucking book,' he said. And I quote.

So I did. Several, in fact. And I emerged from the strange and utterly loopy world of cyberspace theory convinced that in order to understand fully the digital revolution, we would need to see two things very clearly: first, that the computer – no longer just an information processor – was rapidly developing into a sort of deluxe copying machine, increasingly capable of imitating certain aspects of our lives; and second, that a large number of very smart, very influential people believed that this computer copy should, and eventually would, replace the original it imitated. In books and articles, in boardrooms and classrooms, at computer shows and academic symposia, these people argued with positively evangelical fervor for their vision of the computer as God: omnipotent, omniscient, gravid with a New Creation. 'Strait is the gate, and narrow is the way to heaven,' St. Matthew had warned. So widen the bandwidth, the cyberists were answering.

These people, as George Bush might have put it, had the vision thing. In spades. Computers represented the portal to the new Heavenly City; cyberspace would be our new home. According to Michael Benedikt, professor of architecture at the University of Texas at Austin, cyberspace would allow us to make up for the Fall from Eden, to redeem ourselves in God's graces. He was not being ironic. Cyberspace, he explained, would allow us to shed 'the ballast of materiality'; it would be a pure realm – spotless, shining – into which we would be able to escape. And what would we be escaping from? Almost everything, it seemed. The Earth – grubby and all too physical. The limitations of space and time. The body – impure, treacherous, and, most annoying of all, mortal. And on and on. Cyberspace would solve all our problems.

I had assumed that those yearning to escape the world and everything in it (à la Augustine) would have a very special perspective on life in general. And so it was. 'Reality is death,' declared Professor Benedikt, revealing himself as the less-than-perfect dinner companion. His solution to this flaw in the cosmic plan? Cyberspace. And how did the professor envision cyberspace? As 'a territory swarming with data and lies, with mind stuff and memories of nature, with a million voices and two million eyes . . . billowing, glittering, humming, coursing, a Borgesian library, a city; intimate, firm, liquid, recognizable and unrecognizable at once.'[4] Got that?

Like most readers, I suspect, I had no idea what Professor Benedikt might be talking about and this troubled me for a time, until I realized that what I'd been reading was something like the digital equivalent of speaking in tongues. Professor Benedikt and those like him had caught the spirit. Communication was not his aim. Conversion was.

The literature of cyberspace, I now began to see, was

all about salvation. The new, electronic millennium. Transcending time and space, the family and the body. Oh, and sex, too. 'You won't need condoms anymore,' promised Nicole Stenger, a former research fellow at MIT's Center for Advanced Visual Studies. 'Cyberspace will be the condom.'[5]

What did this mean, exactly? It meant, according to Stenger, that physical sex was going the way of the dodo and the ivory-billed woodpecker. That cybersex – a sort of expanded version of phone sex – was the wave of the future: cleaner, simpler, less risky than its messy prototype.[6] It was an interesting vision. If it came to pass, I thought, it would require that we update Hector St. John de Crèvecoeur's eighteenth-century question, 'Who then is this New Man, this American?' In the New Age, apparently, he would be the one in front of the video monitor, one hand on the keyboard, the other firmly grasping his, er, mouse.

But sex was hardly the point. The word *masturbation*, in fact, hardly appeared in the rarefied world of cyberspace, though one could assume that even cyberspace condoms would refer to something, and that cyborgasms, however airy, might still require a little help in arriving. Instead, one found a great deal of talk about computers as the objects of desire. It was all about love, you see. 'Our fascination with computers is more erotic than sensuous,' Professor Michael Heim argued in 'The Erotic Ontology of Cyberspace' – 'more deeply spiritual than utilitarian.' Logging on, he explained, meant taking on the role of the 'erotic lover,' reaching out to 'a fulfillment far beyond aesthetic attachment.' It was all very simple, according to Professor Heim: 'The world rendered as pure information not only fascinates our eyes and minds, it captures our hearts. We feel augmented and empowered. Our hearts beat in the machines. This is Eros.'[7]

But the prophylactic – excuse me, *romantic* – possibilities of cyberspace were just the beginning. According to Stenger, we were teetering on the threshold of a new era. 'It was obvious,' she claimed, 'that an explosion would take place, a Big Bang of the old order . . . based on gravity, history, and territory.' What would this Big Bang of the old order mean, I wondered? Would we all find ourselves afloat in Professor Benedikt's glittering, billowing mind stuff? Just so. Civilization, Stenger assured me, would 'become unbalanced.' She could hardly wait. Cyberspace, she enthused, would be 'the new bomb, a pacific blaze that will project the imprint of our disembodied selves on the walls of eternity.'[8]

The crudity of the metaphor (the 'pacific blaze' Stenger evoked, of course, was the blast at Hiroshima, whose heat was so great that it imprinted the silhouettes of the newly incinerated on the wrecked walls of the city) was characteristic of theoretical writings on cyberspace. It implied a stunning insensitivity to, or boredom with, the merely real world, the world of historical facts and contemporary issues, in which pacific blazes (or the pleasures and risks of human sexuality) had some bearing on actual people's lives. 'If only we could,' Michael Benedikt had written, 'we would wander the earth and never leave home; we would enjoy triumphs without risks, eat of the Tree and not be punished, consort daily with angels, enter heaven now and not die.'[9] As a group, the cyberists seemed to have already ascended. Their perspective was postmillennial, almost hallucinatory. From their vantage, the world seemed vaguely unreal – a half-remembered dream – and *humanity* a term of little consequence.

To say that the real world didn't interest the cyberists,

however, wasn't quite accurate; they didn't *believe* in it. 'What we call reality,' Stenger explained, 'is only a temporary consensus anyway, a mere stage in the technique.' Bodies, Professor Heim claimed, didn't really exist, either: they were ideological constructs – composites of attitudes, beliefs, and preconceptions, themselves dependent on larger economic and political forces at work in the general culture. Nature, too, was merely an idea, a cultural construct. Like love. Or gender.[10]

According to the cyberspace expert Allucquere Rosanne Stone, 'the category "nature,"' rather than referring to anything in the real world, was just 'a *strategy* for maintaining boundaries for political and economic ends.' And what might those be? Why, supporting 'the industries of postmodern nostalgia' (which keep us all hungering after things that never were), for one thing, and for another, maintaining 'our society's pervasively male epistemology' (which demands that we make technology look bad by setting it *against* something wonderful).[11] Nature, in other words, was a patriarchal conceit designed to enslave us to the past and to demonize machines.

At some point, I'll confess, I began to find the whole business more than a little disturbing. Negotiating the electronic precincts of cyberspace, it seemed to me, was a bit like lying down drunk, feeling the room start to turn and spin, and not having a floor to ground you. Or finding yourself in a dream that starts to go bad. There was something vaguely nightmarish about this hunger for transcendence, this lust for dissolution, this utter lack of loyalty to the earth, the body, the human community. Behind the hallucinogenic jargon, the collage of quotes, and the mixed metaphors, I sensed something very lonely. And very frightening.

Was I taking it all too seriously? Looking back from the digital everafter, Stenger had predicted, we would be able to see the divine process by which we'd first 'lost all trace of earth on our shoes.' We would recall how our houses had gradually grown airy and insubstantial, 'whistling with drafts,' and how our families had 'slowly thinned away.' We would remember that moment in time when cyberspace became 'so irresistible that some of the basic functions of human life [fell] off like ripe fruit.'[12] Was there anything in our world, I wondered – visible or not – to justify this kind of prophecy?

Looking around, it seemed to me that there was, that Ms. Stenger's brave new world was not as far off as some of us might have wished. Already, after all, many of us had lost all trace of earth on our shoes. Already – as more and more of us came to spend the hours of our days in the worlds beyond the television and computer screens – our homes were growing airy and insubstantial, whistling with drafts. Assisted by the increasing fragmentation of life in the West – by the loss of community structures, the breakdown of the family, the degradation of the physical environment – we really *did* seem in danger of ascending to some new, electronic reality, of being turned, in Benedikt's phrase, 'into nomads . . . who are permanently in touch.'[13]

It came as something of a shock to me to realize that Stenger and Co., however much they might sometimes sound like Shirley MacLaine, were *serious*; when they talked of their desire to engineer a Big Bang of 'the old order' based on the principles of gravity, history, and territory, they meant it. More important, they had the funding and the technological sophistication to make good on many of their wildest prophecies. By grafting the tradition of millennial dreaming onto both the free market and a powerful new technology, the cyberspace enthusiasts had created something new under the sun. Only half a decade from the turn of the millennium, they were threatening to make it possible not only to sell the age-old dream of the Heavenly City but to rent out space there.

It was more than just their technological sophistication and economic savvy that made them dangerous, however. The cyberists, like all extremists, were products of their time, the children of an increasingly subjective age. To understand them – their airy, relativistic attitude, their complete disinterest in, if not downright animosity toward, the hard facts of history – one had to see them as the intellectual heirs of certain theories that had established themselves in American higher education over the better part of two decades.[14] It was no coincidence, after all, that many of the most ardent theorists (like my lecturer) were academics. Cyberspace, I realized, represented the marriage of deconstruction and computer technology – a mating of monsters if ever there was one.

The connection, once made, was obvious: deconstruction, which began as a method of textual analysis, was all about dismantling the 'apparent' realities or truths of a literary work; the focus was on language's 'unreliability,' the text's 'indeterminacy.' Like a child picking threads from a blanket, the deconstructionist would isolate certain elements of, say, a poem by John Donne, in order to show – often quite reasonably – that all meaning was provisional, that at bottom, the poem was really about nothing so much as its own subversion. The point? Relativism. By exposing the fault lines in any argument, the deconstructionist could show that all hierarchies were suspect, all values provisional, all answers partial – and therefore of equal value.

A high-powered nuisance in the field of literary criticism, deconstruction quickly moved beyond academia, adapting itself – like some opportunistic predator exploiting an eco-logical niche – to the 'texts' of history, identity, and culture as a whole. These, too, were shown to be unreliable, riddled with gaps and inconsistencies, indeterminate to a fault.

The predictable result, as Michiko Kakutani pointed out in the *New York Times*, was 'a cultural zeitgeist in which all truth [was] deemed subjective and all facts . . . made subject to reevaluation' – a climate in which history, for example, as an objective record of events in time, didn't exist. In this New Age, there weren't any facts, just ideologies of the moment; at any given time, the ideologue with the most power and influence got to determine the truth du jour. History, in short – even an event as immutable as the Holocaust – became just a collection of fictions (subjective, indeterminate), a text as susceptible to deconstruction as any poem.[15]

But the spirit of deconstruction didn't stop with the dismantling of history. The self, as something greater than the sum of its parts, was dismantled as well. The human being – and everything she saw and thought and believed – was shown to be nothing more than the product of the ideological filling she'd been stuffed with. One could think of it as a kind of soft version of the Human Genome Project, which attempted to trace every quirk and feature of the human being back to its parent chromosome. Here, too, the trick was to locate the bit, or part; once you'd done that, you understood the person. Did you happen to think that Herman Melville could write? It was because you were a white, Anglo male. Were you troubled by the Serbian genocide in Bosnia-Herzegovina? It was because you'd been weaned on the milk of rationalism, raised in the bland light of Western liberalism and Enlightenment thought.

Like most absurdities, of course, the relativism of the

deconstructionists was based on a number of reasonable and even useful insights – texts, after all, *are* indeterminate; attitudes toward the self *are* circumscribed by ideology; history, or the act of recovering history, anyway, *is* a subjective business.[16] Seen as ends in themselves, however, instead of as means to a greater objectivity, these insights led nowhere. 'Indeterminacy' turned into a fetish, and 'unreliability' acquired its own cult following.

So how did the cyberspace theorists fit into all this? Simple. Like the deconstructionists, the cyberists were enamored of the concepts of indeterminacy and instability; like the deconstructionists, they projected a fashionable, kaffeeklatsch nihilism; like their predecessors, finally, they were morally neuter, less interested in constructing truth and meaning – however provisionally – than in dismantling them.[17]

There *was*, however, one important difference. The deconstructionists had theories; the cyberists had machines. Theirs, in effect, was an *applied* deconstruction. While the deconstructionists could only *argue* that nothing exists outside of us – that reality is just personal perspective – the cyberists had machines that could *make* it so.

In cyberspace, for example, the reality of your experience would change depending on which part of yourself you decided to admit to, and which you suppressed; each time you took on another persona on a computer network (or pretended you were another sex), the cyberspace world would adjust accordingly, proving that just as there *is* no core self, neither is there an objective reality outside the individual mind.

All of which, it seemed to me, left one not-so-small problem: reality. And reality had a bad attitude. It didn't read the assigned texts; it didn't pay attention; it was completely oblivious to the fact that you'd entered cyberspace with

Professor Benedikt, or were now 'rocking and humming in televirtuality,' as Nicole Stenger had put it, in a community of 'highly unstable, hermaphrodite angels.' If the power were to go out as you swam, disembodied, disengendered, through the ether of pure information, you'd find yourself back in the solid world very quickly.

What we had here, I could see now, was self-indulgence raised to the level of a science or, worse, rank escapism masquerading as political engagement. In cyberspace, Stenger had claimed, there would be 'a shifting from the sense of territory, of being an inhabitant of an earthly system of values that includes roots, walls, possessions, toward a radical adventure that blasts it all.'[18] Reading this, I found myself thinking: tell that to Aung San Suu Kyi, only recently released from five years of house arrest in Myanmar. She'll pass it on to the Burmese junta. Or talk to dissident Wei Jingsheng in Beijing, recently released after fourteen and a half years in prison and once again demanding respect for human rights and democracy from the same regime that imprisoned him. Tell the estimated two and a half million Sudanese in imminent danger of starvation that reality is only a temporary consensus. You tell me the mind is a leaking rainbow? I say that from Bosnia-Herzegovina to the Kashmir Valley to south Los Angeles, that airy metaphor is made grotesquely literal every day.

In a world quick to brandish the term *elitist* (our latter-day equivalent of the tar brush and the bag of chicken feathers), here at last was a worthy target. Who, I wondered, were these people talking to? Who, exactly, was this electronic utopia they described intended for? And what about the rest of us? What would we do about all the men, women, or children, of whatever religious persuasion or ethnic background, of whatever class or race or education, who had the misfortune of having to deal with the world as it *is*, not as it *might* exist in the daydreams of Ph.D.s and CEOs with five-thousand-dollar computers? Would bringing the ghettos on-line increase the life expectancy of young black men?[19]

The problem, I realized, was *not* that cyberspace would usurp reality as we know it, or that we would all disappear into some virtual world. The problem, simply put, was that cyberspace would distract us from the job at hand; that, busy blurring the boundaries between biology and mechanics with Allucquere Rosanne Stone, we'd forget that most of the human race was more immediately interested in survival than transcendence; that, as we spent more and more of our time fulfilling ourselves 'far beyond aesthetic attachment' with Professor Heim, we'd forget that the followers of Louis Farrakhan and Tom Metzger and the late Meyer Kahane were going about their business; that, as we wandered through virtual forests, real ones burned.

But wasn't this, after all, highly unlikely? Wasn't it absurd to suggest that the culture of distraction could ever compete with the reality that surrounds us? At one time, I would have thought so. Then I entered the virtual world.

CHAPTER 2

'Springtime for Schizophrenia'

The Assault on Identity

If I hesitated a bit before taking the plunge into cyberspace, I blame technoevangelist John Perry Barlow. 'Nothing could be more disembodied than cyberspace,' Barlow had said, trying to inspire those still hovering, so to speak, on the lip edge of their monitors. 'It's like having your everything amputated.'[1] Wanting to be a good sport, I tried working up some enthusiasm for this notion. Barlow, I knew, was talking about freedom from the flesh; for him, amputation was a metaphor for liberation.

It didn't work. Instead of a vision of the pure realm of the spirit, the image that sprang to my mind was of Dalton Trumbo's tragic hero in *Johnny Got His Gun*: a deaf, dumb, and blind quadruple amputee. Trumbo's hero, it seemed to me, had found himself in cyberspace long before it became a destination of choice. I was in no hurry to join him, metaphorically or otherwise.

That I did, eventually, was due to a book. It wasn't my first choice on the Help menu; I would have preferred a human guide into cyberspace. But each time I'd tried

'F2F' (cyberese for 'face-to-face') communication – asking students or colleagues for assistance – I'd found myself buried under a friendly mountain of acronyms and cryptic code words: 'Be sure to turn on the Local Echo and Wrap Mode options under the Session menu,' a senior member of my department told me. Ah, yes. Of course.

I knew some things. I knew that *Net* was the name given to the tens of millions of computers linked together around the world. I knew that in order to 'talk' to others, or post messages, or access information – the cybernaut's raison d'être – I'd need a modem, which would hook my computer up to the telephone lines. I'd figured out that even though the Internet was the biggest of the networks, there were smaller Nets as well – some linked to the Internet, others not – and that some of these had clever names like KinkNet, FidoNet, and ZiffNet.[2]

I retreated to the local bookstore (apparently still thriving despite the redundancy of paper in this age of transparent information), where I found the computer section hemorrhaging with self-help manuals aimed at 'data. comm.phobes' like myself.[3] A canary-yellow stripe across the top of something called *Net Guide* caught my eye. 'Net Guide is the TV Guide to Cyberspace!' the editor of *Wired* magazine, Louis Rosetto, enthused on the front cover.[4] This seemed to be the ticket.

The foreword, by the ubiquitous John Perry Barlow, cut straight to the chase, skipping E-mail and going straight to eschatology. (The leap from mechanics to theology, I would discover, was a customary one among the cyberists.) The Net, according to Barlow, was not just an expanded version of the old telephone party line, as I had thought. It was 'a state of minds. Or, possibly, in some more realized future condition, The State of Mind.' The Net, Barlow continued, was the current phase of something called the Great Work, which was to be 'the hard-wiring of collective consciousness.' This was 'the end toward which, according to paleontologist-theologian Teilhard de Chardin, the great journey of evolution had been headed all these eons.' At this point, apparently concerned that he might be underselling the thing, Barlow got serious. In all likelihood, he wrote, the Net would 'alter what it is to be human [for the better, I assumed] more than any technological development since the capture of fire.'

The Net, I discovered as I read on, was 'in some loose sense of the word, alive.' As an organism, it was 'a lot like a global nervous system, an almost continuous extension of the wet, gray gauze within the humans who sit at its silicon receptor sites.' Still unsatisfied, Barlow finally fell back on Hindu mythology to make his point. The Net was 'rather like the notion of Indra's Net – an infinite grid of pearls, each of which reflects perfectly the image of every other pearl in it.'[5]

I spent a good portion of the next ten days wandering the dreary reaches of Indra's Net. On the Bulletin Board Services alone, I found (and visited) specialty chat groups like alt.skinheads, alt.skunks, and alt.skateboards. I dropped in on alt.hemp and alt.hangover, pondered the best way to nuke Europe with the boys on alt.nuke.europe, and peeped in (electronically speaking) on alt.christnet, alt.pantyhose, and alt.sex.fetish.diapers. I downloaded pictures of naked blonde women off alt.binaries.pictures. erotica.bl (the *bl* stands for 'blonde'), but balked at alt. binaries.pictures.furry. I had no end of fun on alt.besti-ality.barney, alt.satannet, and alt.evil, on the last of which someone named Vardaman had felt compelled to inform the cyberworld: 'I am on a mission from God. I must edu-cate the styleless monkey boys.' I even visited alt.cuddle, where 'cuddleking' Steve was busy dropping 'thousands of tiny cuddles and huglets' from the 'Huggytank' of his 'Cuddlebomber.' And I disengaged my 'wet, gray gauze' from Barlow's 'global nervous system' convinced that Indra's pearls did indeed reflect one another in the most amazing way (everything I read sounded as though it had been written by the same person) and that, at the end of it all, at the *telos* of human evolution, we just might find (as I did) a catalog of 'crabs questions,' a discussion of Gidget's breast size, and a list of 'vitamins that produce fluorescent yellow urine.'

'It's been estimated,' Barlow had said, that there are 'more words "published" on the Net in a week than are bound into books in the United States in a year. And these words are fresh.'[6] He was half right. There *were* a lot of them: a virtual Alp, in fact. But the vast majority were as stale as week-old bread. The average participant (the high-minded exceptions were few) seemed a fraternity house cliché: an eighteen-year-old male with no sense of time and three burning ambitions: to shock people, to get laid, and to discuss reruns of *Gilligan's Island*. I had spent only a few hours negotiating these self-enclosed worlds, each as exciting as a telephone book left in the rain, before anything resembling an original thought shone like, well, like a pearl from a dungheap.

Trying to reconcile the soaring Chartres of Barlow's rhetoric with the humble mud huts of the BBS's wasn't easy. There had to be more to Indra's Net, I reasoned, than frat-boy pornography and war games and virtual poker. There had to be more to the global nervous system than alt.elvis.king. and alt.drunken.bastards.

There was. A lot more. What I'd failed to appreciate, I realized, was the sheer range and variety of experiences out there. Wandering the Net, I found out, was a bit like looking for a place to eat in a major urban area that stretched from L.A. to Bangkok: fast-food franchises and greasy spoons were everywhere; the three-star restaurants, on the other hand, were both harder to find and (for the uninitiated) harder to get into.[7] Cyberly speaking, I'd been snacking on Chicken McNuggets; the MOOs – the real computer communities – were the Pheasant au Chambertin. I decided to dine out.

My experience in these alternate worlds was both stranger and more disconcerting than I could have imagined. In fact, seen in the right light, some of the things going on in the precincts of cyberspace seemed almost enough to justify the tone (if not the wide-eyed optimism) of Barlow's millennial rhetoric.

What I discovered, obscured by the 'noise' of the Internet, was arguably the biggest subculture in recorded history, a virtual electronic nation. Made up of self-contained communities, this shadow world took up no space, appeared on no census, yet was inhabited, in some very real sense, by people from all over the industrialized world. Every day, millions of individuals were coming home from work or school, booting up their computers, and, in effect, disappearing into other realities.

Some of the communities they were plugging in to (all you needed, again, was a computer with a modem), were very much like real ones: elaborate, hierarchical, bureaucratically complex. And though many consisted of nothing but dialogue – words scrolling across the screen – the MOOs (Multiple User Dungeons, Object-Oriented) were something else again.[8] These, by tapping into a database inside some research computer in California or Seattle, gave the impression of an actual place. One could maneuver through it. Go left to the dining room, say, or up to the bedroom. And the level of detail – though still just a matter of words, of verbal descriptions – was impressive. I found myself in rooms with bookshelves, sitting on sofas next to small mahogany coffee tables with vases stuffed with orange California poppies. The communities themselves had names like Habitat and Lambda House. Some had homes, swimming pools, virtual meals on virtual tables.

And people, I discovered, truly 'lived' in these alternate communities. Many had come to think of them as a second home. They were 'meeting' other people there, taking on other identities, opening businesses, falling in love. They were giving each other cyberspace hugs and kisses. In some of the more advanced communities, they were assembling stand-ins – virtual selves, or avatars – from menus of body parts; these alter egos could then be maneuvered through the virtual world.

And this was just the beginning. What happened when people's avatars were set loose in cyberspace was truly phenomenal. Lawyers opened offices; newspapers with their own editors appeared; people started getting married and divorced. In one system, a group of thieves, apparently taking advantage of the fact that body parts were interchangeable and had market value in the computer-community marketplace, approached newcomers and made disparaging remarks about their heads, offering to get them more interesting ones. When the new arrivals took off their heads, the thieves grabbed them and ran off – to wherever it is that cyberspace bandits go.[9]

There was more; many computer communities were bringing with them some of the more worldly by-products of the real-world marketplace – prostitution, for example. As one of the 'oracles' of Fujitsu Habitat pointed out: 'Fujitsu Habitat's economic dimension makes monetary transactions possible. The client sits on a chair. If he is sitting on the chair and facing in front, the prostitute will stand in front and direct her face toward the chair . . .

it's a position in which the prostitute's face can go to the waist area of the seated client. If payment is made to her account, the prostitute will perform a repetition pattern of head movements, and will work *hard*.' What the oracle was describing, I realized, was a virtual blow job.

To the uninitiated, like myself, all this was enough to bring on an acute case of vertigo. The worlds one entered through the conceptual window of the computer screen, after all, were infinite; there were no borders in the usual sense of the word. Physical space was fluid. So was identity. Lambda House, for example, a cyberspace mansion, was an intricately detailed labyrinth of playrooms and dungeons and forgotten hallways, pubs and pools, and a Department of Psychology for those in need of counseling, populated by entire subcultures whose existence and behavior were limited solely by the whims of their creators.

What did this mean, in practice? It meant that as soon as MOOers typed the code for LambdaMOO into their computers, the following words appeared on the monitors:

> The Coat Closet
> The closet is a dark, cramped space. It appears to be very crowded in here; you keep bumping into what feels like coats, boots, and other people (apparently sleeping).

From the coat closet, they could exit (by typing the appropriate commands) to the Living Room, and from there to wherever they wanted. In one room, people might be having a conversation; they could join in if they wanted. In another, since cyberspace citizens could pretend to be anything under the sun, a four-foot teapot might be discussing Michel Foucault with a bottlenosed dolphin. In still another, someone might be sleeping 'on a soft, beige sofa'; the sleeper would be 'a virtual corpse,'[10] as David Bennahum aptly put it, a cipher for someone not currently logged on to the MOO.

Inhabiting this alternate world, I found, the citizens of Lambda House quickly grew used to a sort of existence by proxy, to negotiating a landscape, and living in a community, that did not exist. For the time of their participation, they experienced what cyberists called 'lucid dreaming in an awake state.'[11] They weren't really here. They were *there*. In cyberspace.

And cyberspace could be a very strange place indeed. In an article for *The Village Voice*, Lambda House citizen Julian Dibbell (aka Dr. Bombay) described a case of rape in cyberspace.[12] On a particular night, apparently, as citizens from New York to Tokyo communed in the Living Room of Lambda House (or LambdaMOO, as the digerati call it), a certain Mr. Bungle went berserk. Mr. Bungle, of course, was just a collection of words, a sort of verbal puppet, but a puppet with the sensibility of a psychopath. Describing himself as 'a fat, oleaginous, Bisquick-faced clown dressed in cum-stained harlequin garb,' Mr. Bungle, beginning at around 10:00 P.M. Pacific Standard Time, proceeded to rape and otherwise violently humiliate a number of other people's avatars. Among his victims, Mr. Dibbell reported, was legba, 'a Haitian trickster spirit of indeterminate gender, brown-skinned and wearing an expensive pearl grey suit, top hat, and dark glasses.' Other victims included Starsinger, 'Bakunin (the well-known radical), and Juniper (the squirrel).'

Not only did Mr. Bungle brutally humiliate Starsinger, Bakunin, and Juniper (one character was made to eat his or her own pubic hair, another to violate herself with a piece of kitchen cutlery); he did it by fashioning a sort of voodoo doll with the power to make them violate themselves. When thrown out of the Living Room, Dr. Bombay reported, Mr. Bungle 'hid himself away in his private chamber somewhere on the mansion grounds and continued the attacks without interruption, since the voodoo doll worked just as well at a distance as in proximity.' Thus, although Mr. Bungle had been kicked out, all present in the MOO at that time had to read the sentence: 'As if against her will, Starsinger jabs a steak knife up her ass, causing immense joy.' This went on, Dibbell said, until Zippy, 'a trusted old timer,' fired a gun of 'near wizardly powers' that enveloped Mr. Bungle in 'a cage impenetrable even to a voodoo doll's powers . . . thwarting the doll at last, and silencing the evil, distant laughter.'

The end of this episode, as Mr. Dibbell's long, articulate, and ever-so-slightly unhinged article made clear, was really just the beginning. Moriah, Raccoon, Crawfish, and evangeline were outraged. Starsinger was 'pissed.' Legba called for virtual castration. The MOO was in an uproar. Eventually, after much hand-wringing and a great deal of talk about censorship and the importance of social control versus First Amendment rights, Mr. Bungle was 'toaded,' that is, kicked out of the community – the virtual equivalent of the death penalty.[13] *Virtual* death, of course, is not like the other kind. By the end of Mr. Dibbell/Dr. Bombay's article, it appeared that Mr. Bungle – or Mr. Bungle's voice, at any rate, or not his voice, exactly, but his written words, his particular sensibility – had returned from the dead. How? The thoroughly toaded Mr. Bungle – or the very troubled soul *behind* Mr. Bungle – had simply set up another account (under the alias Dr. Jest), and re-entered the MOO under another identity.[14]

What was going on here? What was all this about MOO rape and Juniper (the squirrel), and Zippy's gun? And why were Julian Dibbell and the editors of *The Village Voice* spending time on something that was really just an elaborate version of Dungeons and Dragons, a second-generation sword and sorcery computer game? Surely it wasn't the violence: video games for kids (like Mortal Kombat and Night Trap) already offered electrocutions, decapitating uppercuts (you could see the twitching spinal cord dangling from the severed neck), martial arts combatants fond of ripping out their opponents' still-beating hearts, femmes fatales given to roasting their victims, and sorority girls on meat hooks.[15]

The answer, it seemed, was that for the people in Julian Dibbell's community (and tens of thousands like them), LambdaMOO was *not* an electronically generated illusion, but a home; Juniper was *not* a puppet, but a person; and virtual rape could (and did) bring post-traumatic tears to the actual person behind legba, the one sitting at the computer. To *this* person, I realized, legba was real.[16]

How was this possible? Simple. Entering cyberspace required only one thing: that one be willing to take *literally* what was basically one big metaphor. It meant accepting the words 'you enter a blue room with a small table and three wooden chairs' as something more than words on a computer screen. It meant inhabiting a textual world *as though* it were real. In many ways, the MOO was very much like the world of a novel. With one important difference: in cyberspace, the characters could talk back, could take control, could offer you their friendship or humiliate you till you cried.

It was this element of feedback, more than anything else, that provided the alchemy of cyberspace, that seduced the imagination into accepting the fantasy as real. The place was alive, capable of responding to your commands, inhabited by the voices of real people. Accepting these voices as fully human was perfectly normal. *Not* accepting them as human beings, in fact, would be a sign of Bunglelike psychosis.

But here was the catch: the metaphor of the MOO was all of a piece. Accepting Juniper (the squirrel) as a real person meant accepting his world as well. And Juniper's world was a world cut loose from its moorings in reality – a world of rooms within rooms; of innocent objects capable of shearing off the arms and legs of anyone foolish enough to pick them up, leaving them 'twitching excitedly'; of postcards like windows that could drop you, like Alice, into another reality. 'Stare too closely at the postcard of Paris on the fridge,' David Bennahum had written, describing LambdaMOO's Kitchen, 'and you'll find yourself tumbling into it . . . and out onto the Boulevard St. Germain.'[17] In cyberspace you could find hallways with no end, rooms with only three walls, and windows looking out on nothing.

The sense of dislocation this could bring on was considerable. To a 'techno-peasant' like myself (to borrow from the vernacular for a moment), a view of nothing was difficult to conceptualize. 'Nothing,' where I came from, meant an airshaft, a wall, *something*. In cyberspace, however, nothing was truly nothing. The window was open, but there was nothing beyond it, for the simple reason that no one had described it yet. When they got around to it, of course, they might decide to leave it blank.[18]

The result of all this was a landscape seemingly always hovering on the edge of nightmare, a world in which words like *in* and *out*, *near* and *far*, *here* and *there* – though retained for the traveler's comfort – carried no weight whatsoever. When you entered a cyberspace community, after all, you were neither in nor out, here nor there, within the private world nor out in the public realm, entirely present (in real life) nor entirely absent. You were somewhere in between. And in this in-between world, as in a nightmare, what you expected to be true never was; here, reality was forever dissolving into artifice, and patently obvious illusion was taking on a disconcerting solidity. Here, sticks and stones were made of air, but words could definitely hurt you.

Edgar Allan Poe had called this blurring of realms, this sudden suspension of the laws of cause and effect, 'the uncanny.' It had terrified him, and it terrified me no less now that we have the ability to call it up at the touch of a button. Short-circuiting the senses, it seemed to me, was a recipe for madness. At the same time, I had to admit that many others – millions, apparently – were untroubled by all this. They'd made the transition. Habit, the great emollient, had done its work, and the electronically generated world now seemed as real to them as their own homes. It would do the same for me, I was told: in no time at all, I would find myself setting up a date to talk to someone I'd come to care for, or lovingly decorating my cyberroom, or getting together with my fellow citizens for a town meeting. And standing up from my computer, back stiff and bladder bursting, I'd be surprised to find that six hours had elapsed since I'd last checked the time, six hours spent Elsewhere. At this point, cyberspace would seem a reality fully as enveloping – more enveloping, in some ways – as the one outside, the one I now referred to as RL (real life).[19]

At about this time, as I recall, I found myself wondering whether I hadn't been simply imposing my own fears on a neutral medium, whether, in fact, there was anything wrong with cyberspace beyond my own discomfort with it. After all, I remember asking myself, Why not let Dr. Bombay and legba and Juniper (the squirrel) go their own ways? What was the harm, really, in engaging in a sort of electronic masquerade party, if that was what you wanted to do? Why *not* get together with someone six thousand miles away for a drink in a cyberspace bar?

Dibbell himself provided me with the first part of the answer. 'The commands you type into a computer,' he explained, 'are a kind of speech that doesn't so much communicate as *make things happen*, directly and ineluctably, the same way pulling a trigger does.' Computers, he allowed, would soon break down the 'classic liberal firewall between word and deed.' In the world of the MOO, they already had; to be raped by words was to be raped, period. And to have your puppet raped by words was to be raped yourself. 'And thus a woman in Seattle who had written herself the character called legba,' Dibbell argued, 'with a view perhaps to tasting in imagination the deity's freedom from the burdens of the engendered flesh . . . suffered a brand of degradation all-too-customarily reserved for the embodied female.'[20]

Legba, of course, had suffered no such thing. Legba, as even Dr. Bombay verbally pinched himself to remember, was a puppet. The woman in Seattle hadn't been raped, either. She'd been the victim of a sort of high-tech obscene phone call – disturbing, even upsetting, but certainly not rape. That anyone, from legba to Dr. Bombay to Juniper (the squirrel), should equate the two was not only absurd, but dangerous, for it elevated words to the status of acts, and diluted acts themselves into abstractions. One had only to talk to a woman in the 'engendered flesh' who had suffered through the real thing to understand the full fatuousness – not to mention ethical irresponsibility – of the long-winded discussions on the Net concerning Mr. Bungle's 'crime.'

Part of the risk involved in setting up residence in these metaphorical communities, then, was that we might begin to devalue the significance of physical reality. Lost in the strange, hybrid world of the Net, we might come to believe that verbal houses were real houses, that a described beating was the same as an actual one, that Netsex was just as viable as the real thing. In cyberspace, where physical sex – to take just one example – had become a formality whereby any reference to the body elicited the question, which one – real or virtual? it followed that the trials *and* pleasures of the engendered flesh would come in for less than their share of playing time. And this was a problem, not only because it devalued the source of many of our pleasures but because it helped us evade our responsibility as well. From Appalachia to the ghetto, from Guatemala to the Sudan, after all, real bodies suffered. We couldn't help them from cyberspace. Busy arguing away the distinction between words and acts, we were leaving the world to those unsophisticated enough to believe that reality did have something to do with the barrel of a gun.

I'd heard it said, on the Net and off, that the disembodied nature of cyberspace was precisely its strongest suit, that because it was disembodied, it would teach us to value quickness of mind over beauty, wit over physical power, the content of our characters over the color of our skin. By allowing us to live, for a time, in an aphysical world, cyberspace would teach us how to keep the body in proper perspective. By allowing us to meet one another on a purely mental plane, without fear of harm or rejection, the timid would learn to assert themselves, the violent would see the futility of their ways, and the intolerant would come to understand that human beings are more alike than different.

As a dream, it was undeniably worthy. The reality – utterly unanticipated by the idealists who set up the Net – was monstrous: a hybrid world in which every potential virtue became its own dark double; in which freedom became freedom to abuse and torment; anonymity, the anonymity of the obscene phone call; and liberation from the physical body, just an invitation to torture someone else's virtual one. With the checks and balances of the real world barred at the door, all the worst in human nature quickly set up shop. What the planners failed to reckon with, apparently, was the simple fact that freedom exists only within certain constraints, that morality matters only within the bounds of the physical world. There could be no morality in heaven. Or hell. 'In cyberspace,' one enthusiast had written, playing off a well-known horror movie slogan, 'nobody can hear you scream.'

Instead of constructing a republic of the spirit, in other words, an experimental world in which we might all learn to be decent to one another, the founders found themselves presiding over an abstract anarchy. Free to offend others without consequence or shame, cyberspace travelers began to do just that, with a passion. 'Flame wars' – insult fests – erupted across the board; 'netiquette' went down the toilet. 'Everywhere I went in the newsgroups,' John Seabrook wrote in *The New Yorker*, 'I found flames, and fear of flames . . . I'd come upon sites that were in complete chaos, where people had been flaming each other non-stop, absolutely scorching everything around them . . . Sometimes I'd come upon voices that were just howling at the world; you could feel the rage and savagery pouring out through people's fingers and into the Net.' The result, Seabrook noted, were 'messages studded with smiley faces – ":)" – and grin signs "<g>,"' which reminded him 'of the way that dogs have to go through elaborate displays of cringing around each other to avoid starting a fight.'[21]

And flame wars were just the beginning. Laying out the welcome mat for Mr. Bungle had uglier results as well. Freedom from the flesh simply meant that Mr.

Bungle's friends could *virtually* rape and kill, amputate other characters' arms and legs, immolate one another for all to see, describe pet killings in nauseating detail, and so on. 'Freedom from race' didn't stop Mr. Bungle's fellows – to take just one example – from offering Nigger Jokes, a collection of 'jokes' and limericks depicting various ways of killing African Americans, to hundreds of thousands, if not millions, of readers. Some utopia.

Considering all this, I found myself wondering what the appeal could be. So I asked. 'Many of my best friends are on the Net,' someone named Pannikin told me on alt.england (which, as far as I could tell, had absolutely nothing to do with England). But what about the physical side, I asked, treading as softly as possible. What about something as simple as holding hands, or giving someone a hug? Weren't these things difficult to do without? The answer came back almost immediately, clear and defiant. 'I've cyberly hugged and held hands many times,' Pannikin told me. 'The only difference is in cyberspace you can't get hurt.'

But people *were* getting hurt, left and right. It was at this time that I first began to think of the new technology as potentially addictive. Like any good hallucinogen, I realized, the MOO worked by blurring boundaries: between self and other, between the imagined world and the sensual one, between reality and illusion. And if synthetic hallucinogens could be expected to have serious side effects, why not electronically induced ones? After all, drugs – like mescaline or psilocybin – already presented the illusion of seeing or hearing something that did not exist. They were called *psychotomimetic* drugs because they mimicked the manifestations of psychosis, and rendered the individual incapable of staying in contact with reality.[22]

The potentially addictive side of virtual systems didn't

become clear to me, however, until I mentioned my interest in cyberspace to an acquaintance (I'll call him Avram). I'd known Avram for some time. Level, hardworking, with a slow smile and a slightly world-weary demeanor, there was something reassuringly stable about him. Though born and raised in Tehran (he'd emigrated with his family after the fall of the shah), he seemed more content, more rooted, in the New World than I did. When he heard of my interests, he offered to play Virgil to my Dante. Besides being a graduate student in political science, a husband, and a father, Avram, it turns out, was also a long-term citizen in a cyberspace community. I accepted.

I arrived at a private computer room at my university at the suggested time, well after dark, and, after some small talk, Avram booted up the IBM. As we entered the MOO, a list gave the names of those currently present as well as where to find them. Morpho and Nietzsche and Janie were in the Playroom. Brown Baby, Mannish Minx, Slave, and Sylvia's Mother were in the Hall. Avram chose the Playroom, then waved 'hi' to everyone by typing this action in. The response came back almost immediately. 'Morpho waves back'; 'Nietzsche blows Allison a kiss!!'

Avram, I realized, had taken on a female persona, Allison. Though meant initially as an experiment, nothing more ('I was curious to see if I could pull it off,' he said), Avram found that over time, Allison began to take on a curious life of her own. 'On the Net, I *was* Allison,' he told me. 'Everyone knew and responded to me as female.' I asked him whether now, two years after giving birth to Allison, he could reveal his true gender to his friends on the Net. 'I could never do that,' he said. 'They'd probably never talk to me again. They've told me things, as a woman . . .' He shook his head. 'They'd see it as some kind of betrayal.' And he went on to explain how

51

interesting it was to find out what it was like to be harassed
by a man (never considering, apparently, that his harasser
might himself be a woman pretending to be a man).

I watched Avram as he chatted away on the Net.
Characteristically sleepy, even phlegmatic, he suddenly
seemed animated, alert, fully alive. 'Someone's here with
me in RL,' he typed. 'He's interested in VR. Would
you be willing to talk to him?' One of Avram's friends,
Janie, agreed. For the sake of privacy, they decided, the
conversation would take place in Avram's 'room,' with its
Turner prints and rustic decor. I sat down at the keyboard,
careful not to blow Avram's cover and accidentally refer
to him as a 'he.'

The conversation I had with Janie was similar to a
conversation one might have with a stranger in a darkened
elevator during a blackout. There was an odd intimacy
about it. Unconstrained by the social conventions that
come with physical presence, we felt free to get right
to the heart of the matter. In many ways, it was quite
wonderful, and soon I was typing away, laughing when
Janie said something amusing, frowning when I disagreed,
eagerly awaiting her answers to my questions. Only dimly
was I aware of Avram pacing around the room behind me,
periodically breaking in to tell me how strange this was
for him.

I asked Janie about her life on the Net, about the
friendships she'd made in cyberspace. 'I met the love
of my life in VR,' she said. Were they still together?
I asked. 'We meet every day,' she wrote back. I asked
how they'd handled the transition, whether it had been
difficult making the jump from VR to RL. 'We've never
met in RL (sigh!),' Janie answered; 'I don't expect we ever
will. It would be too hard.'

Less than five minutes into the conversation, Avram

abruptly, though politely, took over: 'I guess I'd better get back,' he said. 'I really think I'd better get back . . . I should get back, really.' He was obviously shaken up. Back on the Net, he explained to Janie how weird the experience had been for him, how difficult. 'I feel like I'm going to be sick,' he wrote. He seemed shocked, even embarrassed, by this reaction. I noticed that his hands were shaking on the keyboard. Bewildered, I apologized for any trouble I might have caused him and, soon afterward, left.

Back home, I attempted to figure out what had occurred. Clearly, though I had not been assuming the role of Allison – just using her space in the community to have a conversation, much the way one might take the phone from a friend to talk with a third party – Avram's reaction suggested that my presence in the community for those few minutes had in some way endangered or erased his persona. I had witnessed a digitally inspired case of identity crisis.

Two days later, Avram stopped by the house to tell me what he assumed I already suspected: he and Janie had been having an affair. He was in love with her – with her wit, her charm, her humor. They'd been 'meeting' at least five times a week for almost two years now. And, of course, since Janie had fallen in love with someone named Allison, the relationship had to be lesbian. The experiment of taking on a female role had generated its own reality. He and Janie even had sex, Avram told me, which entailed basically talking each other through masturbation. It was not an uncommon practice among lovers on the Net, he said.[23]

Avram and I talked for some time. What came through most clearly, I think, was the irreversibility of the situation he'd found himself in. He was genuinely in love. He expected that he and Janie would continue to meet on the Net for the rest of their lives, or until that day when one of them failed to log on. And even if the affair were to end, he told me, he could never go back to being just Avram. To come off the Net would be tantamount to killing his persona. Allison was real to him, now. She *was* him. To silence her was unthinkable.

I tactfully mentioned Avram's wife. She knew nothing of what was going on, he said. He felt bad about this. When he occasionally spaced out for five or ten minutes at a time, he explained, it was because he wasn't here, in his actual living room, say, but rather with Janie, in cyberspace.

Subsequent interviews in cyberspace convinced me that Avram's experience was neither atypical nor particularly extreme. Like most of the individuals I spoke to on the Net, Avram did not seem a particularly unstable or conflicted individual. Secure in his sexual identity, he had simply fallen in love. And to fall in love at a distance was nothing special, after all; affairs in cyberspace were simply showing again what human beings had known for a long time: love is not always, or necessarily, physical. But what of the role playing, or shape shifting? The fissioning of individual identity? The psychological investment in surrogate selves?

These, too, it seemed to me, were only variants of something characteristically human. As social animals, we each had an assortment of roles to play – mother, lover, teacher, friend – determined by the company of the moment and the place we found ourselves in. And as for psychological investment, who could deny the tremendous investment made by some individuals in particular parts of their identity: in their corporate selves, for example?

So what made cyberspace different? Simply this: social roles had always been bound and kept in check by the constraints and limitations of the physical world. And this allowed, in most cases, for the development of a relatively uniform ego. Take away those boundaries, however, separate the individual from the physical world, and the ego could refract wildly and at will. Gender switching in cyberspace, I discovered, was routine – not necessarily because the Nets were crowded with men and women yearning to switch sexes (though some would argue just that), but simply because the new medium made 'gender surfing' possible.[24]

Yet – and this was the kicker – it was precisely the strange, aphysical climate that made these identities so easy to create that also preserved them, allowed them to take on a surprising substance, and made them so very difficult to erase. Having created them, individuals like Avram could only watch as their alter egos – supported and reinforced by others' reactions to them on the Net – rose to challenge their primary selves. Avram, in some very real sense, was no longer just Avram, but Avram-Allison.

The revelation was a startling one. Multiple-personality disorders, after all, were disorders primarily because social existence – life within a real-world community – required at least the appearance of a unified personality. What would be the result, I wondered, of a new generation of machines that actively encouraged the development of multiple personalities? Would cyberspace travelers, like actors who have taken on a particularly tenacious role, require psychological counseling in order to leave that role behind? Had a significant portion of the population wandered into psychological terrain beyond their control? Had I glimpsed a major health crisis in the making, a crisis masked, for the time being, by the ready availability of the drug?

Not everyone, apparently, saw this as a problem. In cyberspace, Nicole Stenger promised, multiplied versions of the self would 'blossom up everywhere.' These multiplied selves would be 'ideal, ironical, statistical.' It would be 'a springtime for schizophrenia!'[25] Though I disliked the role of the killjoy in sensible shoes, I found it hard to share her enthusiasm. Multiple-personality disorders were not my idea of a good time; I'd lived the better part of my life in New York City, where individuals suffering from this particular illness were routinely let out on the streets, apparently to effect their own cure. It didn't seem like *their* idea of a good time, either.

Instead of conjuring up visions of the technological millennium, my experience with Avram recalled instead the lecturer whose talk on cyberspace had sparked my interest in virtual worlds. It seemed to me that her prophecies might have been more accurate than even she suspected. Within a generation, she had said, we'd be able to connect our minds to a computer. It seemed we might not have to wait that long. Neural implants might still be some way off, but psychologically, many of us were already securely, perhaps irreversibly, connected. And not just to the machine, but to the marketplace as well.

Each of those surrogate selves – what we might rightfully think of as a sort of shadow population – was held hostage by the monthly phone bill. Bluntly put, Allison (and tens of thousands like her) could live only if Avram and all the other cyberspace citizens out there paid their monthly fees. Don't pay – because you've come on hard times, say, or the rates have gone up – and Allison disappears. Here was a sight that might have made even Orwell blanch: a rapidly growing number of individuals whose identities (or a significant part of them) were dependent on a machine, and whose maintenance they were thereby committed to, for life. Avram would continue to pay his dues. If they were to quadruple next month, he –

and all the others like him – would pay them just the same.

Would all this lead to a new subculture of addicts, I wondered? An army of deprogrammers? A new regulatory agency? Would computer bigamy become legal grounds for divorce? Were the psychiatrists who were already treating 'Net addiction' in New York just the tip of the proverbial iceberg? And how would adolescents – for whom ego formation was still taking place – respond to life in cyberspace? Even Dr. Bombay, after all, had pointed out that Netsex was powerful stuff. If encountered by 'a college frosh, new to the Net and still in the grip of hormonal hurricanes and high-school sexual mythologies,' he admitted, it could 'easily reverberate throughout an entire young worldview.'[26]

But the MOOs, it seemed to me, were most significant as an indicator of what lay ahead. When virtual reality came on-line, Allucquere Rosanne Stone predicted, cyberspace would become 'a toolkit for reconfiguring consciousness'; it would make it possible for a man to be 'seen, and perhaps touched, as a woman and vice versa – or as anything else.' Already, she pointed out, there was 'talk of renting pre-packaged body forms complete with voice and touch . . . multiple personality as commodity fetish!'[27]

Avram's alternate world, I realized, would soon be the Model-T of cyberspace communities. Things weren't going to stop there. And if the current systems had side effects, it seemed reasonable to expect that the more advanced ones would have them in spades; side effects didn't disappear when you doubled the dosage. The push was on, I reminded myself, for increasingly 'real' and eventually inhabitable electronic space. Feedback systems, technological prostheses, even neural implants of some sort, were by no means unthinkable. The groundwork was being laid for a computer-generated reality so powerful, so sensually complete, that once entered, it would be indistinguishable from the outside world. Our avatars, in the not too distant future, would be us. If we weren't careful, we could all wind up raped by Mr. Bungle.

CHAPTER 3

Virtual World

The Assault on Place

Out beyond the looking glass, in the nation's computer science departments and think tanks and corporate laboratories, two kinds of virtual reality are being born. The first is the kind everyone has heard about. It's flashy; it gets all the press. In principle, it will allow us to enter the computer, to immerse ourselves in a computer-generated world. The second, a much sneakier affair, intends to wrap the computer (and its attendant technologies) around us. With *this* kind of virtual reality, you won't need a helmet or force-feedback gloves because your everyday environment will be virtual and the room you inhabit will be a species of cyberspace.

'In the future,' according to Mark Weiser, a computer visionary employed in the Xerox Corporation research labs in Palo Alto, 'the smartness of computers will surround you.' Weiser sees a future in which mobs of quasi-sentient, smart objects, all linked in a seamless web of information, form a sort of machinic ecosystem around us. He sees living houses, each a 'supercolony of semi-smart bits';[1] they'll know who we are, and, yes, we'll be able to talk to them. Just like George and Jane Jetson.

This is the very special world of hyperreality, or augmented reality, or cyberism. Its advocates – from engineers to hackers, from laborers in the fields of biotechnology and artificial life to the high priests of cyberspace – believe that the design of ordinary reality is flawed, and must be put right. How is reality flawed? Well, for one thing, as IBM researchers and psychologists Wendy A. Kellogg, John M. Carroll, and John T. Richards explain, 'objects in our environment are largely "dead" to distinctions we care about. Television sets and stereo systems,' for example, 'are socially insensitive: they don't turn themselves down when we talk on the phone.'[2]

Their organic brethren, it seems, are even worse. Let's face it, says the physicist-author Gregory Stock, 'not all creatures are important to us; there is an immense roster of species that neither affect nor interest the vast majority of humankind.' Not only are the vast majority of the world's species useless, they don't work very well, either. Horses, complains the technoevangelist Keith Henson, can't be switched on and off when not in use. Ken Karakotsios, a former Apple employee, sums up the general discontent nicely: 'The only thing wrong with the universe,' he says, 'is that it is currently running someone else's program.'[3]

What do the digerati suggest? Not, as one might expect, an 'enclosed, simulated reality' – the standard vision of a virtual world apart – but 'a distributed, augmented reality . . . in which cyberization is integrated seamlessly into people's everyday activities, and real-world objects take on virtual attributes and behaviors that support and enhance those activities.' In other words, a *personalized* universe. A universe in which 'dumb' objects, 'electrified with smartness,' entirely subject to our will, form a seamless web around us.[4] In this new world, the environment will be both synthetic and eerily alive; the dividing line between 'the born and the made' will blur. The couch will shrink out of your way like a dog to keep you from skinning your shins, while the cat in the corner will have a patent number on its skull, beneath its fur. Technology will become, as Allucquere Rosanne Stone has put it, the new 'nature' we inhabit.[5]

How crazy is all this? Look around you, says the technoevangelist Kevin Kelly, and you will see that 'the overlap of the mechanical and the lifelike increases year by year.' Already, 'technicians are conjuring up contraptions that are at once both made and alive,' even as life itself (or what we naively used to *think* of as life) yearns for mechanization: 'Under the guise of pond weed and kingfisher,' he maintains, 'life seethes to break out into crystal, into wires, into biochemical gels, and into hybrid patches of nerve and silicon.'[6]

What's disconcerting, of course, is that he's more right than not. The line between the living and the dead *has* been growing increasingly vague. Every day, old frontiers are being erased or pushed back; every year, in laboratories throughout the industrialized world, the edges blur. Already, some of the characteristics of life are being transferred to mechanical systems, even as the engineering of organic systems is progressing at staggering speeds: from baboon hearts to biopesticides to the bovine growth hormone, we're learning to 'hack life.' Soon, the distinction between technologized life (that's us) and living technology (our environment) may be lost forever.[7]

For most cyberists, in fact, questions concerning the border between the synthetic and the natural are already a kind of vestigial limb. There *is* no real distinction between biology and technology, they point out, never was, and any attempt by human beings to argue otherwise, or, worse, to maintain that life is somehow superior to the piston engine, is sheer hubris on our part. Professor Bruce Mazlish of MIT, for example, believes that those still given to this kind of sentimental hoo-ha (primarily 'intellectual Luddites,' 'religious fanatics,' 'humanists,' and 'readers of *The National Enquirer*') are due for a quick dressing-down. We humans, he warns, are not nearly 'as privileged in regard to machines as has been unthinkingly assumed.' When the scales fall from our eyes, we will see that our 'origins are to be found in both the animal and machine kingdoms, with the animal and the mechanical qualities together incorporated in the definition of human nature.'[8]

One can see, of course, how the tabloid-reading humanists among us might be inclined to dismiss this as either anti-elitism run amok (who are you to feel superior?) or a spectacularly literal-minded take on that old 1960s chestnut, *My Mother the Car*.[9] Mazlish, however, is neither easy to dismiss (he's a fellow of the American Academy of Arts and Sciences) nor alone in his vision. More important, his notion that man is unique primarily in his 'attempt to completely eliminate nature in favor of human-made structures' provides theoretical fodder to those doing just that.

At MIT's famous Media Lab, to take just one example, a community of technologists from a dizzying array of disciplines – their numbers include, among others, physicists, mathematicians, neurophysiologists, and experts in animation research, robotics, and artificial intelligence – is busily altering the shape and grain of our universe in ways that even Mazlish might find disconcerting. Funded, to the tune of tens of millions of dollars, by a virtual Who's Who of private corporations as well as the Pentagon's gargantuan Defense Advanced Research Projects Agency (DARPA), they're demonstrating – right now, in hard reality – that the borders of our world are a lot more flexible than anyone suspected, that given enough time and money, almost *anything* is possible.

Almost entirely free of political scrutiny – despite the potentially enormous cultural implications of their work – places like the Media Lab, to recall the words of Ken Karakotsios, are replacing the 'program' of the universe with their own. Led by men like the Media Lab's director, Nicholas Negroponte – technologists with a very real talent for selling their vision – they're quickly and quietly cyberizing the world. And the list of 'business studs' lining up at Negroponte's door, as Steward Brand puts it, is impressive: General Motors, RCA, 3M, all the major television networks, Tektronix, NHK (Japan's public-television network), IBM, Apple Computer, Warner Brothers, Paramount, LEGO, Dow Jones, Time Inc., Polaroid, Kodak, Hewlett-Packard, Sony, Hitachi, NTT (Japan's AT&T), and so on, seemingly ad infinitum.[10]

What Negroponte wants, says Brand in his illuminating book *The Media Lab: Inventing the Future at MIT*, is 'ultra-personalized intimate technology – everything made to order'; the goal at the Media Lab is to 'explore the interactivity between humans and machines down to the finest nuance.' What does this mean in practical terms? It means exploring, for example, the various ways in which the human nervous system might be connected to a computer. It means putting together, bit by bit, what amounts to a machinic ecosystem – a 'forest of machines' that can know you and sense your moods: computers that can look at you and recognize you, phones so sensitive they can pick up 'the information carried in stutters, pauses, gulps, tones of voice' – in short, an infinitely personalized universe, entirely subject to human will.[11]

Where will all this lead? Will the alchemy of the blurmeisters give rise (as they themselves predict) to the emergence of 'mechanical consciousness' or the further evolution of 'man the artifact'? Will 'a pervasive layer of technology' come to separate us from the world we inhabit? Will the natural world be 'managed' like a zoological park, as Stock assumes, and humanity consigned to 'comfortable indoor environments' in which it can 'engage in activity and communication mediated by electronics'? Are 'neural jacks, cyborgian body parts, designer food crops [and] simulated personalities,' as Kevin Kelly suggests, just around the corner?[12] Of course they are, say the cyberists (though some will quibble about the timing). These, and other wonders we can't even imagine, are inevitable. Will we accept them? Of course, they answer; when have we ever been able to resist a new technology? The ball is rolling and no one can stop it. When we are as gods, when we've remade the world in our image, when the microbes replicate just for us, and we've brought the storm to heel, *then* we'll stop.

What drives the cyberists? For one thing, as should be clear by now, a hubris of positively mythic proportions. 'Junior deities, we want to be,' explains Brand. 'Reality is mostly given. Virtual reality is creatable.' (And, he might add, controllable.) Running alongside the god talk, however, is another motivation that periodically surfaces, like some weird leitmotif, throughout the technoevangelist oeuvre: fear and loathing. Fear and loathing of the body, of the natural world, of physical experience in its entirety. According to Professor Mazlish, for example, who is perfectly representative: 'Man's evolutionary drive . . . has seemed to be in the direction of creating his own surround . . . and thus moving further away from his animal nature.' To make his point, he quotes from Yevgeny Zamyatin's dystopic novel *We*, which, he claims (completely missing the import of the term *dystopia*), captures this human aspiration perfectly: 'Man ceased to be a wild animal only when he had built the Green Wall, when we had isolated our perfect machine world from the irrational, hideous world of trees, birds, animals.'[13]

That this irrational, hideous world is on its way out, Mazlish, for one, has no doubt. 'Such are the signs of the times,' he shrugs. Soon, our world will be 'inhabited solely by humans and machines.' Animals, both wild and domestic, will be destroyed. 'To eradicate the animal in himself,' he points out, altogether admiringly, 'man is willing, at least in imagination, to eradicate [animals] in the world at large. And perhaps in actuality.'

Human beings, in other words, disgusted by the body, tired of being ignored by the world of objects, repulsed by the irrational, hideous world, have had it up to here. Being human, they 'do not wish to settle for such a limited condition. They aspire to be angels, if not God.' This sort of thing is in their (our) blood, Mazlish explains. After all, hasn't the Christian religion traditionally placed 'a strong emphasis on escaping the body, and especially abjuring sex'? And aren't we all one in the blood of the Lamb? Well, then, what else can we conclude but that humanity as a whole wants to separate itself from 'its bestial nature and become pure in spirit'? 'Who,' he asks, concluding his case, 'has not felt at times the "foulness" of the body and the desire to shake it off? Has not felt revulsion at the "base" necessity of bowel movements, or perhaps even of sex?' Who, indeed.[14]

Faced with all this, one gropes for an appropriate response. Embarrassment? Disbelief? Surely, we think, Mazlish is speaking metaphorically. And surely the folks at MIT, when they rhapsodize about the possibilities of engineering a synthetic environment, or technologizing our 'surround' to the point of hallucination, don't expect to be taken literally. Right?

Alas, no. They're stone-cold sober. And they don't have much patience with those not tapped in to their vision of the future. As Brand has put it, referring to the new digital juggernaut, 'if you're not part of the steamroller, you're part of the road.'[15] What this means is that if we're to have any say in shaping the world we and our children will inhabit in the next century – if we don't relish the prospect of being rolled over by the cyberists' steamroller – we have to begin paying attention, and fast.

Particularly because, seen in the right light, the cyberists' vision is already coming to fruition. Our world today, by every standard, is more man-made, more synthetic, than ever before. We may not be living in artificial pods quite yet, but increasingly, the sensibility that would interpret that scenario as both grotesque and infinitely sad seems to be fading. In Japan, always on the cybernetic cutting edge, psychiatrists report that workers have begun greeting robots on the production line, and both mountains and beaches have been mechanized and moved indoors: skiing down the artificial hill, breathing the artificially cooled air, you can look up into the steel girders of the 'sky'; lolling on the beach under the artificial sunlight, you and your children can splash in the machine-generated waves.[16]

Seen in historical perspective, in other words, the cyberists make sense: they represent the endgame, the grand finale to one of the great human migrations of all time: the twentieth-century movement into our own 'surround.' Increasingly isolated from ever-greater portions of the external world, our retreat facilitated by machines capable of providing us with many of the things (community, landscape, love, adventure) that only recently required going out, we've been cyberizing with a vengeance. The outside world, if not yet redundant, is getting there quickly.

Already today, for example, by subscribing to Videocycle Tours, 'the fitness enthusiast who is going nowhere' can explore the country roads of Vermont 'without leaving home'; his 'coach and on-screen riding companions' will lead the way on the TV attached to the stationary bicycle's handlebars. After his workout, should his fancy lightly turn to thoughts of love, he can put on an interactive CD-ROM. The sex scenes, presented from the camera on the chest, 'first-person point of view,' will make him feel like he's performing.[17] If cybersex puts him in the mood for a little shopping, he'll soon be able to log on to an Interactive shopping network, which, according to Walter K. Levy, a retail consultant, will enable him to call up a customized selection of merchandise, peruse the options, view individual articles from all angles – or, in the case of clothing, see it on appropriately shaped models – and then order electronically. And he'll be able to do all this, as Levy points out, 'without leaving [his] armchair.'[18]

Absurd? Of course it is. Its absurdity, however, only accents the significance of the phenomenon it represents. For hundreds of millions of individuals throughout the industrialized world, life has collapsed (largely, if not entirely) into a series of interior spaces, all more or less alike: the home, the car, the office. For tens of millions more, entertainment has become increasingly synonymous with spectatorship (or voyeurism), abstract communication has become the norm, and firsthand experience has joined the list of endangered species. Like hermits peering out of their respective windows at the passing world, we're being reduced to watching the world through the electronic windows of the television screen and the computer monitor (for which we can now buy fake stick-on window frames complete with trees, flower boxes, and swept-back curtains). And we're getting used to it. Sending E-mail to a friend or watching elms shimmer in the bright fall sunshine on a Nature Company video, we realize, may not be the same as talking face-to-face or walking in the woods, but, increasingly, we seem willing to accept that. 'It's the next best thing to being there,' as the old AT&T ads used to say.

AT&T, of course, doesn't say that anymore, which itself says a great deal. It suggests that the *real* significance of our retreat from the world may be located not so much in the technology that makes it possible as in the revolution in attitude that makes it appealing. That revolution, like so many before it, has been a matter of language, of reinterpreting certain terms to create a new reality. AT&T, it would seem, doesn't use the old slogan because 'being there' no longer means what it used to.

By the time the corporate slogan had evolved into 'reach out and touch someone,' the assumption that physical proximity to someone was more valuable than talking over the phone was no longer a given. Talking on the telephone, it seems, is no longer 'the next best thing to being there'; it *is* being there.

What we have here, if nothing else, is a fascinating case study in how the power of language can alter perception.[19] We are seeing, after all, a blending of reality and metaphor: a willingness to equate the *real* highway with the digital one, physical space with cyberspace, real communities with virtual ones. Was this demotion (and abstraction) of the physical world somehow consciously orchestrated? I doubt it. Is it being actively encouraged today because the new formulations translate into mind-boggling profit for those who will furnish our new digital lives? Count on it. As more of the hours of our days are spent in synthetic environments, partaking of man-made pleasures, life itself is turned into a commodity. Someone makes it for us; we buy it from them. We become the consumers of our own lives, a recession-proof market if there ever was one. 'I believe,' says the computer-assisted design specialist John Walker, that 'in the fullness of time, every object in the world, manufactured or not, will be modeled inside a computer. This is a very, very big market. This is everything.'[20]

What it comes down to is this: the digital revolution represents a potential $3.5 trillion market. Vitally important to the success of that revolution is our willingness to move indoors, to renounce the external world (where so many things are free, after all) in favor of the internal one (which can be commodified to the heart's delight by selling us substitutes of the things we've given up). And how do you facilitate the movement from public space into the private home? Simple. You reinterpret the meaning of private and public. You redefine inside as outside, absence as presence, abstract space as Cartesian and three-dimensional. Along with Allucquere Rosanne Stone, you call technology the 'new nature.'

All of which, one would agree, is a pretty effective way to break down the defenses of those inclined to resist the digital zeitgeist. You're not alone, the argument goes; you're connected. You're not isolated in your room, tapping on a keyboard; you're in touch, linked up, wired to the world. How do we explain the new fear of being left behind, of being insufficiently wired? How do we explain the growth of what can only be described as bandwidth envy? Simple. When the virtual becomes the real, then the computer becomes our window onto the world, and the bandwidth the door by which our friends come to visit.

We'll naturally do everything (buy anything) to keep that window open. In time, we may come to fear its closing like death itself.

All this may explain how we come to find ourselves where we are – that is, on the cusp of a New Age in which more and more of us happily equate real life with abstract existence. What it does *not* fully explain is our rush to embrace the new thinking, our apparent lack of allegiance to the physical world. What it does not answer is why we should *want* this new world. And want it we must. After all, new technologies (and new definitions of old concepts) can go only so far by themselves. They need our help. Without it, they would die on the vine. If enough of us said 'no, thanks,' and went outside for a bike ride, or a walk in the woods, or up to our bedrooms to make love, Videocycle Tours and Nature Audios and Netsex would go the way of Scent-a-Rama and 3D glasses. As would many of the projects at the MIT Media Lab. What explains the attraction?

The short answer is paranoia. As everyone who reads a newspaper or partakes of the evening news already knows well, it's a dangerous world out there. Parks are bad. The streets are worse. Sex is dangerous. Post offices, apparently, are death itself. But fear, legitimate or otherwise, is only part of the explanation for our withdrawal from the outside world, and not even the largest part. As it turns out, it's not so much that we're afraid of what's out there as that there's no there out there anymore.

Not too long ago, on an episode of *The Simpsons*, the community's television sets are simultaneously turned off. The effect is immediate. To the swelling strains of the opening movement of Beethoven's 'Pastorale,' children – dazed, blinking in the sun like mice coming out of winter hibernation – begin to emerge from their houses.

In seconds, they are running through the fields, flying kites, building tree houses, swimming in pristine creeks. At the family dinner table that evening, the kids are flushed, tired, and happy. Bart is bursting with news. 'And you know what else?' he says, holding his arms a yard apart. 'We almost caught a catfish *this* big!'

The scene is hilarious, of course. It works well, and not just as a parody of that brand of hokey American nostalgia captured in everything from Norman Rockwell paintings to Kozy Kountry Kitchen Kitsch, but as a wonderfully reflexive takeoff on our often overblown fears of the television set itself. Kill the tube, we are being told, as we sit watching, and ye shall inherit the Earth. The Simpsons' brief sojourn in the outside world, however, is effective for another reason as well. It cuts close to the bone. Like a lot of good humor, it's funny because it hurts. And it hurts, basically, because the communitarian vision beneath the parody is something both strangely familiar and increasingly foreign. By turning the actual agrarian past into a Tom Sawyer fantasy, *The Simpsons* underscores how far from that world we've actually come, how terribly antiquated, even fantastic, the world of creeks and horseshoes and catfish has come to seem.

This sense of disconnectedness from our own past, in turn, helps explain why we seem so willing to isolate ourselves from the external world, why we seem so incapable of resisting the encroachment of abstract space on our lives. Simply put, we're retreating inside because the world outside our homes has less and less to offer us. Going fishing, for most of us, is not an option, not necessarily because the fish might give off a disconcerting glow, but simply because chances are good there is no stream or lake near us, and therefore no fish. We live, many of us, in communities whose planners clearly had little or no interest in integrating the outside world into the lives of future residents. In most of these places, if the TVs were suddenly to break down, you could hum Beethoven's Sixth until the cows came home, but there would be no stream, no tree houses, no lawn big enough to play horseshoes, and no meadow for the cows to come home to.

My morning commute offers a dozen examples. From the highway (one of the major West Coast arteries), I can see community after community, each stuffed with identical (and very expensive) houses on a quarter of an acre or less, each with a two-car garage. The postage-stamp lawns are manicured, perfect, and empty. Looking at these communities, one thing is utterly obvious: no life outside the home is possible here. There is no playground, no park, no field or meadow. Children don't play ball in the streets; couples don't scandalize grandmothers by kissing too long and passionately in the shadows of the trees (there are none); neighbors don't talk or even argue. The only option, if you want to go out, is to take a car. So what do the people who live in these communities do? What else *can* they do? They live inside: watching television, listening to their home entertainment systems, playing computer games. When they go out, they do so mainly to go in: to a mall, a store, a movie theater. As Gregory Stock aptly puts it: 'No wonder the emotional links between humans and the "natural" environment are weakening; an ever growing fraction of human experience is in an entirely different realm.'[21]

Our movement inside the home, in other words, is to a great extent an environmental issue. As the natural world disappears from our lives, we are forced inside. Our move indoors, however, marginalizes the physical world still further, in the process cutting us off from what's left of the life we once knew: a life rooted in a *physical* community and a particular, local landscape. To the cyberists inclined to characterize that vision as hopelessly romantic, a yearning for some idealized, Jeffersonian past, I'd simply reply that arguing the importance of the physical world is not utopianism but simple sanity. To think that we can do without, that we can substitute virtual alternatives for the real thing, is madness.

And yet that is precisely the point being made, explicitly and unabashedly, by the cyberist vanguard: Why go out when you can stay in? You say you want to fly a plane? Log on. Like fish? We'll sell you digital ones. Worried about AIDS and STDs? Miss September will take her panties off just for you. (You say it's not the same, that masturbation, however interactive, is still the next best thing to being there? Give us time. We're working on that.) Why go through the trouble of moving your actual, imperfect body through physical space, when you can 'get there' instantly? Why put up with flawed reality, when you can engineer your own 'surround'? Embrace the machine – it's your kith and kin, your soul, your savior.

Strangely enough, to bolster this vision, cyberists like to fall back on literature.[22] Their favorite, judging by the frequency with which it is cited, is Samuel Butler's satirical novel, *Erewhon*, in which the author takes on all manner of Luddites and states (they love this quote): 'There is no security against the ultimate development of mechanical consciousness, in the fact of machines possessing little consciousness now.' It's a good quote. It works well. But if works of literature are to guide us into the cybernetic future, I have a better one in mind.

In 1928, E. M. Forster sat down to write a science fiction story. It was not his usual fare. Forster, the author of *A Room with a View*, *A Passage to India* and *Howard's End*, among others, was more typically interested in anatomizing the deficiencies of the English middle class than in predicting the future. Forster's sensibility, however, had picked up a trembling in the cultural chrysalis. Troubled by the increasingly machinelike dynamic of twentieth-century life, instinctively attuned to the forces that separate people from one another, Forster noted the signs of the times, then looked into the future. Apparently he didn't like what he saw.

A dystopic nightmare fully worthy of Orwell, 'The Machine Stops'[23] opens in 'a small room, hexagonal in shape, like the cell of a bee.' The woman who lives in this room, Vashti, shops by phone, orders food by phone, gives lectures to an audience she can see and hear without leaving her room. She's pathologically afraid of direct experience. In her world, direct observation, physical space, the unmediated event, have all been banished. Her room – an underground bunker linked to others through a sort of computer fully equipped to compensate for the outside world – is a self-enclosed universe: 'though it contained nothing,' Forster tells us, 'it was in touch with all that she cared for in the world.' Nature has been removed from human life. 'She made the room dark and slept; she awoke and made the room light; she ate and exchanged ideas with her friends, and listened to music and attended lectures; she made the room dark and slept.'

Into this self-enclosed world (his image appears on a blue, TV-like plate) comes Vashti's son, Kuno, a rebel, a malcontent, who lives in a room just like hers in the Southern hemisphere. 'I want you to come and see me,' he says. Vashti, at first, doesn't understand. 'But I can see you,' she protests. Kuno, however, doesn't want to see her through the offices of the machine. Absurdly, he wants more. 'I see something like you in this plate, but

I do not see you,' he says. 'Pay me a visit so that we can meet face to face, and talk about the hopes that are in my mind.' Eventually, though already anticipating 'the terrors of direct experience,' Vashti agrees to go.

The journey itself is an ordeal of uncontrolled events. Though transportation is rapid and painless, though the shock of the new has been largely neutralized (all the world, Forster tells us, now looks roughly the same), though nature has been tamed utterly, other sources of distress have arisen to take their place. When Vashti stumbles, for example, the stewardess, still possessed of a 'certain roughness and originality of manner' from having to deal with people, behaves barbarically: forgetting that people no longer touch one another, that the custom has 'become obsolete,' she reaches out to steady her, then instantly apologizes for not having let her fall. When a man accidentally drops a book (a relic from the Age of Litter), all the passengers are disquieted. The passage is not mechanized; the floor can't pick it up.

Face to face with his mother, Kuno tells her of his crime. In this Age of the Machine, in which direct experience has been demonized and the natural world rendered obsolete, Kuno has been to the surface. His rebellion knows no bounds: 'We say space is annihilated,' he argues, 'but we have annihilated not space, but the sense thereof. We have lost a part of ourselves.' Kuno – young, aggressive, curious – is determined to recover the physical world. 'Man is the measure,' he claims, to his mother's horror. 'Man's feet are the measure for distance, his hands are the measure for ownership, his body is the measure for all that is lovable and desirable and strong.'

Crawling upward through the machine, Kuno claims to have stuck his head into the darkness of actual night. 'I seemed to hear the spirits of those dead workmen who had returned each evening to the starlight and to their wives, and all the generations who had lived in the open air. . . . I felt, for the first time, that a protest had been lodged against corruption, and that even as the dead were comforting me, so I was comforting the unborn. I felt that humanity existed . . . and that all these tubes and buttons and machineries neither came into the world with us, nor will they follow us out, nor do they matter supremely while we are here.'

Vashti, struck dumb by her son's confession, leaves him to his fate, knowing that 'on atavism the machine can have no mercy.' She returns to her cell in the hive, unshaken in her devotion to the Machine. The room hums, the machines do their work. Swaddled in comfort, she resumes the abstract life she briefly interrupted.

Forster's story concludes like something out of the Book of Revelation. The consensual illusions, the glowing televisionlike plates, the remote music – at first gradually, then with terrifying speed – begin to shut down. The bunkers go dark. The machine on which humanity has come to depend as a substitute for the world simply stops. Groping her way into the outer passageways, Vashti finds her son, who has come to see her in the final hour. As they hold each other, an airship crashes downward through the human hive, exploding as it goes. 'For a moment,' Forster writes, 'they saw the nations of the dead, and, before they joined them, scraps of untainted sky.'

I confess that I've never been particularly interested in science fiction. Faced with Forster's Dantesque vision, I find myself wanting to qualify, to distance myself from a parallel that seems at once too obvious and too reductive. It's so unabashed, after all, so transparently biased in its allegiance to the physical world – the actual landscape, the human touch. Forster's world is not ours, I want to say. *We* don't live in bunkers, after all. *We* still meet one another in real life, touch one another, make love to one another.

But I can't do it. Everywhere we look, it seems to me, Forster's world is beginning to emerge like the pattern of wallpaper coming through the paint. Seventy years ago, Forster placed his heroine at the center of a human hive. Today, the technologists use that very metaphor to describe the interlinked hive nature of the Net. (The cover of Kevin Kelly's book *Out of Control*, for example, features drones flying from an apartment building in which each window/cell is a computer screen.) Seventy years ago, Forster wrote: 'Under the seas, beneath the roots of mountains, ran the wires through which they saw and heard.' Today, the prophecy has been fulfilled. Our 'wired planet,' Kevin Kelly notes, is rapidly becoming 'a torrent of bits circulating in a clear shell of glass fibers, databases, and input devices.' Another example of Kevin Kelly's New Age hyperbole? Not at all. AT&T, I read in the paper, is laying fiber-optic cable around the continent of Africa.[24]

And the parallels, of course, don't end there. In Forster's story, cyberspace reigns supreme; representations have come to be regarded as superior to the originals they imitate;[25] technology has become a deity that increasingly demands fealty from its many acolytes, a deity, in other words, beyond its creators' control.

As we continue to hurtle toward the technological millennium, Forster's story appears both prescient and genuinely frightening, its lessons uncannily apropos. What its characters did not consider, it seems to me, was where the changing times would lead; how 'way leads on to way,' as Robert Frost put it; how certain choices inexorably lead to others, perhaps less welcome; how habit tends to be self-perpetuating; how, finally, the psychological strength required to live fully in the real world can wane and atrophy, much like muscles and ligaments left too long unused. Forster's fiction describes an incremental apocalypse; increasingly enervated, impatient, and irritable, humanity entrusts everything to the machine. And the machine stops.

In our lifetimes, it's just getting started.

CHAPTER 4

Highway to Hive

The Assault on Community

World building, most would agree, is a reflexive business; altering our 'surround' means altering ourselves. This raises some interesting questions. If, as the digerati contend, our world is soon to mutate beyond our recognition, what kind of human (or human community) will come out of the mix? What will the lives of individual men and women be like after the digital revolution has run its course?

To be fair, these are questions the cyberists themselves never tire of asking – and answering. So what *will* our lives be like in the digital New World, according to those in the know? Improved in every way, say the rank-and-file boosters on the Net. We'll be able to do everything by remote; the world will be our oyster. Glorious, say the mid-echelon enthusiasts. The New Age will elevate the human spirit and lead to the solution of social problems. Define *human*, say the true digerati. Define *world*.[1]

Which leaves the rest of us, wetted fingers to the air, testing the digital winds. That the times they are a-changing, there can be little doubt. Already climbers on the go are placing phone calls to Los Angeles from the summit of Mt. McKinley in Alaska, hikers are using hand-held global positioning devices and computerized altimeters to plot their location, and the Motorola Corporation's Iridium system of communications satellites is making it possible 'to make a phone call – or to be beeped – from anywhere on earth.' Bored with the increasingly wired wilderness, meanwhile, former outdoors types are taking to the wilds of cyberspace, losing themselves in 'the neck of the Internet called the World Wide Web, pointing and clicking a trail through a maze of hypertext documents and digital pictures.' And this, we remind ourselves, is just one wavelet in the sea change taking place, just one yellow brick on the road to digital Oz.[2]

What's really in store for us in the new millennium? Where will the changing times, left to unfold according to the cyberists' blueprint, lead us? No one knows, seems to be the usual answer. Better, therefore, to wait and see. Which sounds reasonable enough. While we're waiting, however, we can get a pretty good idea of where things are going simply by looking closely at the two great metaphors spawned by the digital revolution thus far: the information superhighway and its newer, more aggressive successor, the digital hive.

Why turn to literary tropes for answers? Because metaphors, whether they reveal the truth or obscure it, always have a great deal to say about those who use them. Plotting our trajectory from highway to hive gives a sense of the direction our guides have in mind for us, of what they consider important, and what they're prepared to discard.

Digitally speaking, the storming of the Bastille occurred on January 13, 1994, when Vice President Al Gore traded in his politician's shovel for a modem and symbolically broke ground on the new data highway: he held the first interactive computer network news conference. Everything went swimmingly, more or less: the glitches were minor, the VP was able to 'preach the techno-gospel' to 'the electronic supplicants trooping into the White House,' as Peter H. Lewis of the *New York Times* put it, and everyone went home (or logged off) convinced that the 'global information infrastructure,' loosely known as the information superhighway (still more loosely as the Infoway, the I-Way, or the Infobahn) would soon be an essential part of our lives.[3]

Looking at the Associated Press photograph of the event, the first thing that arrested my attention, besides Gore's exemplary posture, was the huge photograph of the Earth that served as a backdrop. So dominant was this image, in fact – and so closely cropped was the photograph of the VP in action – that Gore and his computer seemed strangely unmoored, floating off into deepest space like Bruce Dern and his electronic humunculus in the 1968 cult film *Silent Running*.[4] The Texas-sized symbolism was clear: here, obviously, was an event of global, nay, universal, importance.

And who could argue? Daily, it seemed, the roar (or buzz) of the data highway had been growing louder. Since 1992 alone, the number of newspaper articles mentioning the information superhighway had risen over 2000 percent, nearly every one filled with the kind of positive-thinking, forward-looking, onward-marching rhetoric usually reserved for re-election campaigns and times of national crisis.[5] In the nation's bookstores, meanwhile, experts were arguing that logging on to a computer network was actually a kind of 'conversion,' and electronic communication, a species of 'communion'; that universal access to information would empower the weak and hamstring the tyrants of the world; that, thanks to the wonders of digital communication, the meek would finally inherit the Earth. 'Blessed are the poor in data, for they shall have universal service,' read an italicized box in a *New York Times* article.[6]

Clearly, here was a phenomenon to be reckoned with, a phenomenon that dipped boldly into the soup of metaphors we had learned to identify with the spirit of America: the open road, the new frontier, the untrammeled wilderness, the liberating wonders of high technology – all glazed, as it were, with the mild light of God's approbation. The data highway, we were being told, marked the dawn of a new day for humankind; it was a 'wonder,' a 'miracle,' sure to 'elevate the human spirit and lead to the solution of social problems.' In due course, the vice president assured us, it would promote economic growth, foster democracy, and 'link the people of the world,' bathing us all, willy-nilly (every last mother's son, apparently) in the warm milk of human kindness. One world, one love.[7]

Though it seemed mean, even vaguely unpatriotic, to quibble, I couldn't help wondering how, exactly, we were going to pull off this miracle. It was not that I lacked enthusiasm for Mr. Gore's transforming vision; I was all for building castles in the air (à la Thoreau), then putting foundations under them. It was just that in this case, the gap between vice presidential rhetoric and Third World realities, to my mind, resembled a certain canyon in northwest Arizona. How was a computer in every home in Rwanda, I wondered, going to help stop the slaughter or ease the poverty – prerequisites, one might think, to such Western niceties as free elections or the establishment of a free press?[8] How would access to the digital highway mellow out the Khmer Rouge and the Sendero Luminoso? And who was going to buy the world's tyrants and tyrannized – many of them illiterate, desperately poor – the means to their salvation? Al Gore? Bill Gates?

The claims being made for the digital highway, I recalled, had been made for the automobile, the telephone, and the television, too. Had they worked? In the squatters' settlements in Mexico City, to take just one example, makeshift shacks with corrugated iron roofs now featured television antennae attached to iron pipes or odd pieces of lumber. This fact, curiously enough, hadn't convinced the reigning International Revolutionary Party (PRI) to relinquish its stranglehold on Mexican politics. Nor had it done much to end endemic official corruption, state control of the press, or the existence of 'virtual' opposition parties manipulated by the regime. Underemployment, poverty, malnutrition, and illiteracy had increased dramatically. Despite the liberating wonders of the *telenovela*, piped water remained a dream for millions.

What had happened? Why hadn't the oppressed masses, enlightened by their access to the 'planetary information network,' taken to the streets demanding representational government? It was a mystery, a mystery likely to continue, I thought, when fiber-optic cables, running alongside open sewers, replaced television antennae as the new harbingers of democracy.[9]

Out on the digital highway, however, set against the time-honored American tradition of technological utopianism – which had once allowed us to read the locomotive as an agent of God's will – concerns of this sort were armadillos in heavy traffic.[10] It was morning in America again, and naysayers and 'gloomy-bumps' (as my son's preschool teacher would put it) need not apply. Once the mythic energy of the highway had been tapped, I realized, the nation had gone on automatic pilot. Here, suddenly, was Captain Kirk and the crew of the Starship *Enterprise*, boldly going where no man had gone before; here were all those virile young men and nubile young women we had watched over the years on our television sets, spinning down highways or caressing chrome; here was the lone individual driving his Mustang (four-legged or Ford hardly mattered) into the nation's future, determined to have it all and then some. On the digital open road, down on the new Route 66, all that was best about America was taking on new and luminous form.

Or maybe not so new. What we had here, as all the talk of space and freedom made clear, was not just the highway to heaven, but the second coming of the American frontier – an 'infinite' and 'permanent frontier,' as the co-founders of the Electronic Frontier Foundation explained. This new territory, just like the old one, would allow people to begin again. And again. It would make it possible for them to leave their pasts behind, to appear and disappear at will.[11] And, unlike the older generation of frontiersmen, this new generation of computer cowboys would be able to explore a new world, hack their own communities out of the digital wilderness, hell, even be dangerous, in their not-so-dangerous way, and still be back in time to take out the garbage.[12]

In fact, with no Pacific to block us, no soil to exhaust, and no indigenous cultures to 'civilize' out of existence, the new, improved version of the ol' prairee would be a good deal all around. The 'land' would last forever; democratically minded, like-thinking colonies would form when and how they wanted and disband when they no longer felt the need for one another's company, and free of the risk and responsibility of physical presence, we would all blossom into a nation of unique, fearless, freethinking individuals. Declawed and defanged by aphysical space, we would attain the New Canaan at last.[13]

I saw it a bit differently. Beneath the hodgepodge of symbols and the high-powered hype, I saw a technology with the power to erode what little individualism we had left. Instead of the great flowering of diversity supposedly awaiting us out on the digital frontier, I saw tokenism masking a vast sameness.[14] Where others saw the promise of America, I sensed a tremendous force for conformity – the dark side of e pluribus unum. The highway, to my mind, was a symbol less of the freedom and self-expression awaiting us in the digital future than of the homogeneity we had already achieved in the present.

How would the digital highway change our lives? It seemed logical to ask how the *actual* highway had changed us. Which brought me back, curiously enough, to the Gore family. Gore's father, it turns out, had built highways, too. As one of the principal architects of the national highway system back in the 1950s, he had helped replace the meandering back roads of America with the no-nonsense, high-velocity interstates we had all come to know and love. In a sense, he'd expanded the nation's bandwidth; the new roads carried more traffic, more efficiently, at greater speeds. If they blurred everything in between out of focus – the faces of the locals, the contours of the landscape, the regionally specific details of daily life – well, that was the nature of the beast: quantity over quality, speed over substance.

The parallel, father to son, actual highway to Infobahn, seemed instructive. Al Gore Jr. was clearly following in Dad's footsteps, in a virtual sort of way. His contribution, the digital highway system, was *also* going to be wider and more efficient. It, too – like the first highway system – would carry more stuff, faster. It, too, we were being told, would be a boon to democracy, 'connecting' all those still outside the Net – and too unenlightened to grasp the handicap this implied – to the great commercial web of the nation. It followed that just as Dad's highways had erased many of the particulars of place, Al Gore Jr.'s digital highway would complete the process, displacing the physical world altogether – abstracting travel to communication, and physical space to a metaphor.[15]

Like father, like son. I would have found it touching, all this passing on of the flame, were it not for the losses we'd incurred along the way. And the losses still to come. For just as surely as Al Gore Sr.'s highway system had helped homogenize the American landscape, replacing the distinctive color and lingo of regional culture with the ubiquitous ugliness of the corporate strip, his son's electronic highway would make us blander still, sacrificing a *different* kind of regionality – the 'regionality' of race and gender and age and opinion – to the needs of the all-blurring, eternally inoffensive Netsoul. And thus homogenized, our edges rounded and smoothed, we would fit more easily into the pegboard of authoritarian control.

Was I being unfair, I asked myself at some point? Was I tarring the digital highway with Orwell's brush for no reason? Al Gore, after all, seemed an eminently decent man, as did many of the others who had nothing but good things to say about our mass migration onto the Infobahn. Was I – could it be? – just an old-fogey libertarian incapable of appreciating, at the advanced age of thirty-six, the many wonders that lay ahead?

In my hour of uncertainty, a new breed of bold and unapologetic digerati – bearing a new and more revealing metaphor – came to my aid. Straightforward and direct, uninterested in pacifying *anybody* with the old lies about self-expression and freedom, they quickly and efficiently laid all my doubts to rest. Forget all that guff about the

open road, they said. Forget all that talk about individualism and empowerment on the I-Way, about mom-and-pop
stores on virtual main streets and cozy communities off
the Infobahn. Forget about the Lone Ranger on the new
frontier. In the New Age, even the myth of individualism
will die, and the only community will be the community
of the hive.

At the heart of the cyberists' vision – the true cyberists'
vision – hums the *digital hive*. What is it? It's the real
Dorian Gray behind the digital portrait: an intelligent,
unapologetically messianic, ferociously unsentimental prediction of what the human community will (and should)
look like after the digital revolution has run its course.
A passionate argument for the beauty of the mob, the
virtue of the collective over the expendable individual,
it is also one of the more stunning attacks on what we
might loosely call humanist values to come down the pike
in quite some time. Which is not to say that in its purest
form, the cyberists' self-described in-your-face vision can't
also be quite entertaining. It can, indeed. At times, in fact, it
offers as much fun – there's no way to put this delicately –
as some of the aphorisms of Pol Pot in the 1970s or Hitler's
more memorable pronouncements in *Mein Kampf*.

Reduced to its barest essentials, the metaphor of the
digital hive argues that in the very near future, human
beings will succeed in wiring themselves together to such
an extent that individualism as we know it today – an
illusion in any case, we are assured – will cease to
exist. What will take its place? The great truth of our
collective identity, made clear and apprehensible through
the offices of that 'global mind,' the Net. Absorbed into
'the anonymous nature of the mob,' we will quickly and
gladly relinquish our will, our intelligence, and our beliefs

to the glory of the hive. For its part, the hive will do what it has to; unknowable, godlike, a 'global superorganism,' it 'will not consider our individual fortunes any more than we ourselves think of the many cells that die when we go for a hike and get a blister.'[16]

What will it mean to be part of the global superorganism? What will the hived world be like? Unlike anything we've known or dreamed, according to the visionaries. As the human race mutates into the human hive, apparently, the course of events will quickly spin beyond the control of anyone or any group of individuals; life will be chaotic, 'headless,' utterly 'anarchic.' A scary thought? Only to control freaks and those incapable of appreciating the 'incipient techno-spiritualism of the New Age,' the digerati maintain. The hive, you see, will take care of us. It will know what's best. 'Irredeemably social' and 'unabashedly of many minds,' it will possess 'an intelligence that none of its parts does.' And, just like a real beehive, it will decide 'as a whole when to swarm and when to move.'[17]

And what of us, the new drones? Ignorant, docile, governed by 'the Invisible Hand' of the hive, we will disappear in a rapture of submission. Reduced to the level of guppies in a farm pond or bats on the wing (the cyberists' metaphors, not mine), we will let the mob, the hive, guide our way. 'As we wire ourselves up into a hivish network,' says Kevin Kelly, whose voice is perhaps the most eloquent on the virtues of obeisance, 'many things will emerge that we, as mere neurons in the network, don't expect, don't understand, can't control, or don't even perceive.' But this, he explains patiently, is 'the price for any emergent hive mind.' Besides, he adds, what kind of control can we expect, considering the extent to which the 'collective hive mind transcends [our] small bee minds?'[18]

*　　*　　*

To the unhived, admittedly, a little of this can go a long way. What, we may ask, does any of this have to do with anything? And why should we – as men and women, not four-winged, stinging insects – pay attention to anything as patently silly as the digital hive? Why not let the hive hum on in the minds of the digerati and go about our business? Why not leave the Invisible Hand to drum its Invisible Fingers, and worry instead about H. G. Wells's morlocks, or the fate of the Starship *Enterprise?*

The answers to these questions, though admittedly difficult to swallow at first, are clear: because the Invisible Hand, as corny as it may sound, is no less absurd (or mystical) than the icons of power used by authoritarian regimes in the all-too-recent past; because the digital hive, alas, does *not* hum in the minds of the digital elect alone; because Wells and the writers of *Star Trek*, unlike the digerati, used the vehicle of science fiction to affirm the intrinsic worth of human virtues like compassion, intelligence, and tolerance; and because, finally, the whole elaborate metaphor of the global superorganism, like most monstrosities – like the Third Reich, say, or the utopia of the proletariat – is based on a solid foundation of reasonable premises and hard facts.

Human beings, the digerati point out – to take just one example – do not exist singly, in a vacuum. Like all living organisms, they are part of a web of mutually supportive relationships. A reasonable point, and a true one. So far, so good. Using this biological truism as a kind of ideological spring, however, the digerati then catapult themselves (and us) into the neobiological void. Our interdependence, it turns out, has nothing to do with the biota we inhabit; it's interesting only insofar as it exposes the Big Lie: individual identity.

'There is no "I" for a person, for a beehive, for a

corporation, for an animal, for a nation, for any living thing,' declares Kelly, in no uncertain terms. In fact, 'the apparent individuals that life has dispersed itself into are illusions' – taxonomic errors. What's real, then, we might ask? The mass, the hive, the headless swarm. The intelligent whole made out of moronic parts, as the computer giant Martin Minsky of MIT explains. Superior, uncontrollable, damn near sentient in its own special way, this mass organism (author Gregory Stock personifies the thing, calling it Metaman) will take us '*beyond* Homo sapiens' to the next great stage in human evolution.[19]

Which leaves only the small matter of cost to be discussed; great stages in human evolution, it seems, aren't cheap. So what's the price tag on the emergent hive mind? You guessed it: an indeterminate number of drones. It's regrettable, but, alas, inevitable, Stock points out, that 'at times, painful social trauma and individual tragedy [will] attend Metaman's spread.' A high price to pay? Hardly, says Stock. The upheavals of any particular age, he reminds us, are 'but a stage in humanity's journey,' and we must remember that individual tragedy – like roadkill receding in the rear-view mirror – will diminish in importance as we speed into the postindividual world.

In the digital future, in other words, the human hive will not mourn its drones any more than a beehive thinks to count its dead. Though the unhived may feel momentarily saddened, they will have to wean themselves of such useless sentiments by concentrating on the larger picture and bearing in mind that civilization 'is remarkably resilient,' that 'even history's darkest episodes [Stock mentions the Black Death, the worldwide influenza epidemic, and the two world wars] . . . each began to fade from humanity's collective memory' within 'a few generations.'[20]

Of course, fussing over such things as epidemics and wars, if we are to believe the digerati, will soon be a thing of the past, in any case. 'As Metaman becomes a creature of interacting organizations rather than individuals,' Stock explains, 'more and more human activity will lie beyond the range of our natural empathies,' and 'human values [will] have to adjust – sometimes drastically – to the new realities of the human environment the superorganism is creating.'[21] Having adjusted, apparently, we'll understand the transcendent glory of the whole and the necessity of sacrificing to its welfare.

A good thing, too, because the new realities, judged by today's standards of empathy, will not be pretty. 'The birth pains of Metaman,' Stock points out, 'may well devastate certain cultures and populations [never mind which ones] in parts of Africa, Asia, and South America.' Wrenched by the arrival of modern technology, they'll either adjust or go under. Global problems like overpopulation, meanwhile, will be dealt with quickly and efficiently. How? Stock isn't quite sure, but assures us that the trains will run on time. Metaman, after all, is a resourceful deity. Perhaps, Stock speculates, he'll develop some form of today's Australian rabbit virus, 'a human contagious flu-like infection which [will] render large parts of the population unable to conceive children.'[22] Which parts? Stock doesn't say. It's not his place, after all, as a cell in the new body politic, to question the all-knowing wisdom of the Net.

Had enough? Sorry. Not only, says Kevin Kelly, will the hive destroy once and for all the myth of the individual – who, we recall, never existed to begin with; it will wean us of our sentimental overemphasis on the welfare of the human species as a whole and (why stop there?) even that 'swarm of non-mechanical things' we call life.

Living things, he explains, are overrated. Walking up

a windblown ridge near his home, he notes 'where deer have matted the soft grass into a cushion,' itemizes (quite beautifully) the trampled stems of wildflowers – 'the lupine, blue-eyed grass, thistle and gentian' – and finds it all wanting. 'I should be impressed,' he writes. 'But what strikes me as I sit among the two million grass plants and several thousand juniper shrubs, is how similar life on Earth is.' 'Life can't fool me,' he says. 'It's all the same, like those canned goods in grocery stores with different labels but all manufactured by the same food conglomerate.' This vision – epiphany, really – of 'life as a networked thing – a distributed being' moves him considerably. 'We are of the same blood, you and I,' he chants, quoting 'the poet Mowgli. Ant, we are of the same blood, you and I. Tyrannosaurus, we are of the same blood, you and I. AIDS virus, we are of . . .' But you get the idea.

Back in the bosom of civilization, Kelly reflects on his sojourn in the wilderness and comes to a number of startling conclusions. Life, he realizes, 'is a transforming flood that fills up empty containers and then spills out of them on its way to fill up more. The shape and number of the vessels submerged by the flood doesn't make a bit of difference.' (To whom? one can hear the bits of 'distributed being' ask.) Life, he decides, quoting the British inventor and atmospheric chemist James Lovelock, 'is a *planetary-scale* pheonomenon,' immortal, and any attempt to narrow the aperture to anything less than this godlike perspective is an exercise in self-delusion. What of men, women, families, nations, the whole damned human race, as Mark Twain put it? Pay them no mind, says Kelly. 'Despite the rhetoric of radical environmentalists,' he assures us, 'it is beyond the power of human beings to wipe the whole flood of life off the planet. Mere nuclear bombs would do little to halt life in general, and might, in fact, increase the nonhuman versions.' Which ones? Well, ah, how about rocks? Rocks, Kelly maintains, are also a form of life. A very 'slow' form, true, but still.[23]

How, we may wonder, do we make our way back from all this – from a future made safe for rocks and roaches – to something resembling the world we live in? What bearing, if any, does it have on us today? And why shouldn't we assume, while learning about the hidden benefits of nuclear holocaust, that Kevin Kelly, executive editor of *Wired* magazine (described in Kelly's own book as 'the hottest and hippest magazine of the 1990s – an in-your-face four-color manifesto of digital culture and computer visionaries'), isn't simply being outrageous because outrageousness sells magazines and books?

I asked myself these questions over and over as I made my way through the digerati canon. The more I read, however, the more clearly I came to realize, first, that there's more to the concept of the hive than we might think and, second, that it wouldn't much matter if there weren't. Why? Because what's important about the hive is not the imminence of the brave new world it predicts, but the sensibility of those desiring it. Even if the notion of the global superorganism were fantasy and nothing more, we would have to take note of those trying to make it real.

But it's not fantasy. Increasingly wired together, economically and emotionally tied to our fellows in ways we ourselves barely understand, plugged into a worldwide information grid capable of supplying us with 'live' reports from Bangladesh or sub-Saharan Africa at the touch of a button, we really do seem to be moving toward some as-yet-undefined collective state. Already, as Stock rightly points out, our technologies have bound us into 'a dense network of communications links and trade systems. . . . Without noticing it, we walk above pipes and cables, beneath airplane flight corridors and satellite broadcasts, through radio and television transmissions.' In fact, 'if all communication . . . left behind a conspicuous threadlike trail, soon everything and everyone would be ensnared in a dense tangle of fibers.' Increasingly drawn together by the web of our own technologies, Stock argues, we're 'evolving' away from our earlier, individual natures – which were locally defined, rooted in place – toward a communal, mass self, global in scope.[24] Wind down the metaphor a bit, deliteralize it a little, and you see that he's right.

In fact, as the realm of individual action grows ever smaller, as the group event of yesterday – the ball game or county fair – grows to national and even global proportions (on any given weeknight, the statisticians tell us, fully half the population of the United States is watching television), the cyberists' notion of a global organism, a human hive made up of hundreds of millions of interlinked computers, comes to seem increasingly sober.

Already today, Kelly points out, 'every fact that can be digitized, is. Every measurement of collective human activity that can be ported over a network, is. Every trace of an individual's life that can be transmuted into a number and sent over a wire, is.'[25] Already the human community moves and swarms as the tides of market and media 'information' dictate. You think the human hive is a harmless abstraction? Think again. Hell, we're halfway there already.

What the issue comes down to, then, is not whether or not we are wiring ourselves up into a hivish network – we are – but whether this is a good thing or a bad thing. The digerati, clearly, think it's terrific. 'Metaman,' sings Stock, 'is thriving,' and we must do what we can to aid him in his 'inexorable march' into the future.[26]

I, for one, would rather set up a good roadblock. Why do I say this? Because all the worst we've been – from the Mongol invasions to Majdanek to My Lai – we have been as groups, and because the human hive, as a concept, threatens to destroy the great counterforce to these periods of mass psychosis, namely, the individual's ability to feel compassion, loyalty, and love for others. It's all quite simple, really. For me, despite our viciousness, all hope – such as it is – is located in the individual man or woman; he or she is the beginning and the end; from the love that one person can feel for another, all the larger forms of love – the love of humanity, for example – derive. The digerati, on the other hand, despise and distrust the individual. He disgusts them. Which is why they're ready to sacrifice the individual to the will of the mob, or replace him or her with something better: the Omega Man, perhaps, or Gregory Stock's *Homo comboticus* ('computer robot').

Look at the average human being free of the sentimental claptrap that has traditionally obscured your vision, the digerati will argue, and you'll see that he's not much to write home about. What is man, asks Professor Bruce Mazlish of MIT, but a bipedal mammal/machine noteworthy primarily for its self-loathing (this, says Mazlish, explains our desire to make ourselves into new, artificial creatures by plucking our eyebrows, shaving our faces, and cutting our hair), its delight in inflicting pain on other members of its own species, and its fear of death? Why not do better, he asks? Is Mazlish unique, in either his assessment or his candor? Not at all. 'Man to my mind is about the nastiest, most destructive of all the animals,' the technovisionary Warren McCulloch is quoted as having said some years back. 'I don't see any reason,' he added, 'if he can evolve machines that can have more fun than he himself can, why they shouldn't take over, enslave us, quite happily.'[27]

This vein of repulsion (and self-hatred), when combined with the cyberists' reforming spirit, makes for a troubling combination. On the one hand, the digerati sing the praises of the digital blender, of pureeing ourselves into one, indistinguishable mass; on the other hand, they want to be the ones to push the button. Which doesn't seem fair. If we're all to leap into the hive together, that's one thing; if Kelly and Co. are telling *us* to leap while they watch, that's quite another.

And yet that seems to be precisely the case. In a quote widely associated with the opening of the real computer revolution, Steward Brand wrote, 'We are as Gods, and might as well get good at it.' This was like catnip for the digerati, who, twenty years later, still haven't tired of associating themselves with deities large and small. For Mazlish, the enlightened among us will be as the heavenly seraphim, far removed from the fallen world of men. For Kelly, it's back to being God. From recreating the creation to giving machines the 'elixir of life,' he wants to have it all. 'Stripped of all secondary motives,' he writes, 'all addictions are one: to make a world of our own. I can't imagine anything more addictive than being a god.'[28] None of which, one must admit, sounds particularly dronelike.

So what's going on? How do we explain the schizophrenia here? One way might be to point out that candor has its limits, and that those desiring to play the wizards in the new computer game called life are smart enough to know the value of indirection; better, in other words, to temper the god talk with long testaments to the value of self-abnegation.[29]

A more charitable explanation – noting their lack of artifice, their wide-eyed reformer's zeal – might portray the digerati as nothing more than political naifs: hip, post-modern urbanites – chock-full of partially digested Foucault and crème de Derrida – who don't think twice about combining the nitrogen and the glycerin of absolute power and absolute subservience for the simple reason that these concepts mean nothing to them. Immersed in hyperrealities, well fed but world-weary, they're too busy showing off the latest nihilist couture to consider the impact of their words.

But even if this latter explanation were to turn out to be true, and I don't believe it will, it would hardly matter. Either way, the effect would be the same, the spirits being disturbed – whether out of malice or stupidity – equally deadly. And to appreciate the full threat of the digerati vision, all we need to do is bear in mind that we've seen the human hive before, and recall what happened when it last decided, like 'a single sentient organism,' to swarm.[30]

Behind Kevin Kelly's ultra-hip rhetoric, I hear the dull drone of 50,000 at Nuremberg, the buzz of excitement suddenly rising to a roar, then subsiding again like a wave. I see again the excited yet uncomprehending faces, the young men in knee socks, like drones around the perimeter of the hive, bobbing up and down for a better look. I see the rank and file of the human hive, captured forever in Leni Riefenstahl's brilliant propaganda footage, 'ready to swarm at a moment's notice.'[31] And I think to myself that Mr. Kelly and his fellow enthusiasts need to rethink their vision of the future, and that the rest of us need to start paying attention.

CHAPTER 5

A Republic of Illusion
The Assault on Reality

Understanding the strange, wonder-working technologies of the digital revolution requires seeing them, above all, as the natural, even inevitable products of a culture in which 'the replacement of reality with selective fantasy,' as the architecture critic Ada Louise Huxtable once put it, might well be the national pastime.[1]

At bottom, after all, digital technologies are all about the strange alchemy of simulation; the technovisionaries may talk about the virtues of burying every man, woman, and child under continents of instant information, but what *really* gets their juices flowing is not information, but, strictly speaking, disinformation: the dream of the perfect fake, the undetectable forgery. As Dr. Brenda Laurel, a self-described research artist in virtual reality has said, 'Everybody wants to create something so intense it would make you lose your balance.' What 'everybody' wants, in other words, is an illusion so perfect it will fool us – like birds crashing into windows – into mistaking it for the thing itself.[2]

In a culture less alienated from itself and the world around it, in an age less immersed in the hyperrealities of television and advertising and that delinquent product of their union, political imagineering, all this would hardly matter. But ours, to put it delicately, has always been a culture more than casually acquainted with illusions.

Long before the advent of computers, reality in America was being shaped and 'spun' by the special effects of rhetoric; long before the Orwellian adjective *virtual* slipped into the national lexicon, before *morph* became a verb familiar to every schoolchild in America, the hard facts of territorial expansion, for example, had been morphed into the shape of manifest destiny. It was something we had a knack for. A gift, even. In America, reality's dominion was always under siege, its power continually undermined – as a generation of cultural historians has shown us – by a people uncommonly good not only at manufacturing illusions, but at believing in them.

The cyberists' hunt for the perfect copy, I am saying, makes sense in a culture in which the boundary between fact and fiction has been, as the philosopher Umberto Eco put it, 'contaminated,' in a nation whose defining and most internationally familiar landmark is arguably *not* the dome of the White House, but Mickey's Magic Kingdom.[3] Virtual reality is logical in the context of a virtual age. None of which, of course, makes the new technologies any less dangerous. Already barely hanging on to objective reality, daily dragged downward by the accumulated weight of the unrealities we consume, we're in no condition to absorb the shock of a new generation of illusion-making technologies that threaten to send us straight through the looking glass.

According to some, of course – and their case is a good one – our fingers slipped years ago, and the only question remaining is how far we'll fall. In a brave and brilliant article anatomizing the virtual realities of

American politics, Michael Kelly has argued that ours, in effect, is already a republic of illusion, a country run less by elected officials than by the men and women who package and sell them to an electorate increasingly willing to believe – in the scripted words of the tennis star Andre Agassi – that 'image is everything.' Politics in America, Kelly claims, 'is less about objective reality than virtual reality,' and this sad state of affairs, far from being limited to that Oz on the Potomac, our nation's capital, is representative of a culture in which 'the border between reality and fantasy has been lost, a culture that has produced Oliver Stone as a historian, Joe McGinniss as a biographer, Geraldo Rivera as a journalist, Leonard Jeffries as a geneticist and Barbra Streisand as an authority on national policy.'[4]

Kelly's argument, however daring, has already begun losing ground to the runaway momentum of the new age.[5] Today, facing a new breed of aggressive, reality-busting technologies, we need to consider not just the virtual realities of politics, but the politics of virtual reality.

What do I mean by the politics of virtual reality? Nothing more or less than the political impact of a school of technologies that threatens to permanently blur the line between what is real and what is not. But why political, specifically? Why not cultural? Admittedly, the distinction is a fine one.[6] I choose political because I believe that the digital revolution, in its heart of hearts, is about power in a way that cultural conversations are not, and because our mass descent into virtual reality, though clearly a cultural affair, nonetheless leads to a *political* reality as startling as it is ugly.

In the world of virtual realities, of course, the relevant and the ridiculous are forever joined at the hip: in cyberspace communities, sociopaths come disguised as giant blenders or six-foot spuds; in Washington, political rhetoric blurs with the soaps; and in Colonial Williamsburg, our descent into illusion is announced by eighteenth-century ladies in hoop skirts and Reeboks.[7] Which can make it difficult to know where to start. If I'm right, however, and if all examples culled from the culture of illusion are at bottom part of the same thing – our contemporary assault on reality – then we can start anywhere, confident that all roads eventually lead to the same destination, and that digital fish have as much to say about our direction as a culture as, say, the latest examples of David Gergen's political spin-doctoring.

What are digital fish? *Digital fish* (for the sake of those still blissfully ignorant of the world of computer-simulation games) are simulated fish found on a variety of computer programs now available for home or office. For 24,800 Japanese yen (roughly $240), you can bring home a diskful and plug them in to your computer. What do they do? Short of rising to a fly or sizzling under a squirt of lemon, just about everything.

In a program called Aquazone, for example, they grow, mate, and reproduce 'over a period of months or years if you choose to draw out the drama,' all the while swimming about in 'a virtual aquarium so real,' as Kim Eastham of *Wired* magazine has pointed out, 'that the only thing missing is the smell.'[8] Do they scatter if you tap on the glass of your computer screen? Not yet. Soon, we are assured. On the other hand (check it off in the verisimilitude column) they can die. Whether through neglect or stupidity, you can murder them as easily as their RL brethren. If you feed them too much or too little, if you go away on vacation without arranging for someone to take care of them, if you don't give them their medicine or maintain their 'water' quality or baby them in a hundred other ways, they'll go belly-up at the top of your aquarium/computer screen.

So how real are they? On the one hand, of course, they're not real at all. They're computer simulations – imitation fish in an imitation tank, the finned equivalents of the gluttonous little Pacman symbols that used to munch their way through computer mazes in the days of yore. On the other hand, they *seem* real. Very real. 'The fish, water, and environments are so lovingly crafted,' says Eastham, 'an untrained eye would take an Aquazone for the real thing.' The 'water' behind your computer monitor seems translucent; the fish swim in the smooth, tail-flicking manner of real fish. You want to touch them. Which is the whole point, after all. 'I didn't want to make something just pretty,' says Ron Dicarlantonio, the program's designer; 'I [wanted] them to be alive.'[9] And on some level, he succeeded.

Am I saying that Ron Dicarlantonio did Genesis (or Darwin) one better? No. Fish are fish, and Dicarlantonio's fish are not. But this did not seem to matter much to the couple who called the company in tears when their fish, as the saying goes, bought the farm. For them, as for many if not all of the thirty thousand other Aquazone hobbyists who didn't necessarily mourn their virtual guppies but only talked to them, fed them, and rejoiced at the birth of their fishy babies, these fish were real. All of which says less about the reality of virtual fish, it seems to me, than about people's emotional vulnerability and the possible psychological side effects of electronic illusions seemingly real as life, yet neither.

A tempest in a teapot, or a virtual aquarium, at any rate? It might be, if the attempt to transmute life into digital code stopped with fish. But that hasn't happened. Moving on from virtual fish – you won't find the Holy

Grail in a fish tank, after all – the digerati have stepped up to . . . you guessed it, virtual kids. Another simulation program, Princess Maker 2, allows you to raise a virtual girl from a 'homeless, nameless waif' to 'a sweet, well-adjusted 18-year old.' It also allows you to screw up in all sorts of parental ways. If you feed her rich foods, for example, her cholesterol level will rise dangerously; if you undereducate her, she'll come to a bad end; if you push her too hard, ditto. 'Your virtual girl,' reports Eastham, who seems to have a penchant for these things, 'can take 15 different part-time jobs, from babysitter to bar hostess. You make the choices and pay the consequences. If she gets too stressed out between work and school, you can send her to a sanatorium for a nice rest.'[10]

Described by its producer, Akai Takami, as 'a long-term game where you make a commitment and create your own world,'[11] Princess Maker 2 is Aquazone without the technologically sophisticated graphics; in other words, even though you can mess up your adopted child as easily as you can your virtual guppies, the kid, for the time being, looks like a cartoon. What will happen when she looks real enough to touch? Or when the wizardry of animatronics gives her expressions, and texture-mapped skin, and the ability to respond to your moods – to comfort you, or cry? What will happen when force-feedback technology allows you to stroke her hair? All these things, after all, are already possible.[12] Will we be able to check into that virtual sanatorium along with our troubled offspring? Who knows? Already, Takami claims, distressed users have called to tell him that their 'little girl ran away from home,' and to ask what they could do 'to bring her back.'[13]

Computer simulation games, of course, are hardly limited to programs that allow adults to raise digital kids; in fact, it's hard to think of a sphere of human activity that *hasn't* been simulated. Some simulation games, like Forever Growing Garden, or Davidson's Zoo Keeper, allow kids (real ones) to explore various natural habitats – rainforests, grasslands, mountains – and visit the animals that live in them. It also allows them to visit those that *don't*, that is, those that have gone extinct. Instead of exploring a local farm pond (or catching praying mantises in the park), today's eight-year-old can explore on her computer. Instead of keeping and taking care of a pet, she can spend time with her electronic pet on her computer. Instead of visiting real animals at a zoo (itself already a kind of simulation), she can visit the dodo and the passenger pigeon (and others sure to follow in their path without our very real intervention) on the computer. All this may have its advantages – no smashed aquariums, no dog hair on the sofa – but what it lacks is inestimable: in a word, reality. The plants, the animals, the ecosystems inside the computer may seem real, but they ain't.

Does it matter? Of course it does, and in more ways than one. On the most practical level, the ease with which these games blur the line between appearance and reality, the ease with which they are able to capture their users' emotions, raises some interesting questions about other computer-simulation programs, the vast majority of which, after all, are less interested in growing things than in skewering them. Or shooting, bombing, or burning them. Will the ten-year-old who mangles and mutilates his victims on the latest version of Doom – an unabashedly violent simulation game marketed by its twentysomething creators very much like a drug – get as attached to his slasher persona as his mild-mannered counterpart does to his virtual fish?[14] Will the realistic screams and 'aggro' endearments ('Fuck you! Eat shit, you little fucker!' and so on) coming from players immersed in today's computer worlds become cries of real pain, real fury, as the quality of the illusion grows? There's no reason to think they won't.

What's significant here, it seems to me, is not the simulation, but our willingness to buy into it; whether we're growing tomatoes or slicing our way through a crowd with a chainsaw, after all, we're buying into a fake, and that says something about us and our relationship to reality. Simulation games are important, in other words, because they are part of something larger: the wholesale blurring of the line, as Eco put it, between the original and the representation. By their very nature, they suggest the extent to which reality, increasingly displaced in our lives by the authentic reproduction, is beginning to lose its authority.

If counterfeit technologies were limited to the world *inside* the computer, if dealing with them meant nothing more than dealing with the psychological side effects of raising virtual fish or virtual kids, or living in virtual communities like LambdaMOO, for that matter, they'd be less of an issue. But they're not, and we can't. And this, I believe, is the point. Just as cyberists hope to turn our world – outside the computer – into a kind of cyberspace, so the illusioneers or imagicians or whatever we choose to call them are introducing their hallucinations into the culture at large. Unsatisfied with hacking reality on the inside, they're after bigger game. Why? Because, as the press critic Morris Wolfe recently put it, 'it is easier and less costly to change the way people think about reality than it is to change reality.'[15]

There is no particular border, after all, between the illusion of reality presented by digital fish and the illusion of reality presented by a digitally altered photograph. The culture of simulation is all of a piece, and whether we find our forgeries in a computer, a newspaper, or the culture at large makes little difference.

Above my desk, tacked to the wall, are two clippings. One is a reprint of the famous photograph of Churchill, Roosevelt, and Stalin taken at Yalta in 1945. Standing directly behind them, in shirt-sleeves, is Sylvester Stallone. Funny in a small way, amusing in its irreverence toward the major players of twentieth-century history, even witty in its blurring of politics and popular culture, the picture is so technically striking as to bring on a kind of historical vertigo: the grain is consistent, the shading, just right. Stallone himself – heavy-lidded, musclebound – seems impressed by the gravity of the moment; one imagines him turning to Stalin after the shutter's release, saying, in his trademark basso Brooklynese, 'Yo, Joe, about that occupation zone in Korea . . .'

My other clipping, while technically similar, leaves out the element of the absurd. It shows two images, before and after manipulation. The 'before' photograph shows former Secretary of State Jim Baker sitting on a couch, with Foreign Minister Raul Manglapus of the Philippines at the opposite end. Baker, while smiling at the camera in the foreground, is half-turned toward Manglapus. He seems excessively formal, like an awkward suitor with a guilty conscience. His left arm is resting on a cushion between them. In the 'after' photo, an image of Saddam Hussein, taken from another photograph, has been inserted between Baker and Manglapus. Perversely enough, this doctored image, at least in terms of body language, seems more natural than the first. Baker's left arm now rests naturally across Saddam's shoulders. His right, which before had seemed to be gesturing for some inexplicable reason toward the cushion's center, is now quite naturally, even warmly, indicating his friend Saddam Hussein for the benefit of the press.

Why do I keep these clippings? Not, first of all, because they are in any way unique; the photo of Marilyn Monroe on the arm of Abraham Lincoln in a recent issue of *Scientific American* (Marilyn looks thrilled, the president, thoughtful) would have done as well. As would a hundred others. Nor do I keep them because the technology they reveal is all that new or startling; image manipulation, as the digerati will tell you, is yesterday's news. I keep them because I find them so emblematic of the increasingly slippery world we inhabit, a world in which 'convincing visual evidence,' as William J. Mitchell of MIT has pointed out, 'can be faked with ease.'[16]

Once upon a time, Mitchell notes, one could assume that photographs were 'causally generated, truthful reports about things in the real world.' No more. 'Digital imaging,' he says, 'has subverted these certainties,' and as the flood of visual information coming to us in digital format continues to rise, 'we will have to take great care to sift the facts from the fictions and the falsehoods.' Will this be possible? Unlikely, Mitchell admits. Already, counterfeits have entered the market undetected, and the American Society of Magazine Photographers, in a desperate measure, has asked its members voluntarily to identify forgeries.[17] Will we bother to ferret out the forgeries, even if they are detectable? Perhaps. More likely, though, we'll accept doctored photographs the way we accept simulated fish, unconcerned that our faith in what our eyes tell us is being undermined by technologies capable of faking life, or forging history, perfectly.

Am I saying that once upon a time, before the advent of image-manipulation techniques, all was as it seemed? Of course not. Propaganda is as old as language, the original photograph at Yalta was staged, and one of the reasons Baker seems so ill at ease in the 'before' picture on my wall is that the first photo doesn't depict 'reality' either, but rather the virtual reality of the photo-op.

But it's one thing to leave something out, or to rig the meaning of an image by presenting it in a particular way; it's quite another to recreate the image itself. This is what image manipulation is making possible, and this, as Stephen D. Isaacs, the acting dean of the Columbia University School of Journalism, has said, is 'the ultimate journalistic sin because it [tampers] with reality at a time when images, sometimes more than words, are the message.'[18]

Admittedly, this is ripe territory for technophobes. It doesn't take a paranoiac, however, to sense the potential for disaster in a counterfeit-producing technology that traffics in the single most influential currency of our day: the visual image. If we lived in a time when other forms of information – the print media, for example – retained their authority as the prime sources of information for the majority of people, image manipulation might be less of an issue. But we don't. We live, instead, in an increasingly visual age, consumers, not of life, but of representations of life; of movies, videos, and commercials; of media events and reenactments, which present us with images (in Michael Benedikt's memorable phrase) 'of life not really lived anywhere, but arranged for the viewing.'[19] And this, to put it bluntly, makes us vulnerable. With nearly 50 percent of us functionally illiterate, and 90 percent of us listing television as our primary source of news, we're ripe for the picking.[20] Or the manipulating, as the case may be.

A subject already dear to the hearts of popular novelists and Hollywood producers – a fact not without its irony –

the fear of image manipulation has lately entered the ranks of official phobias, stamped and sanctified by vehicles like Michael Crichton's xenophobic novel/screenplay *Rising Sun*. One doesn't have to plow through Crichton's painful clichés (lustful senators, dead blondes, deceitful Asians armed with inscrutable technologies, and the like), however, to appreciate what may come to pass when the will-to-propaganda enters the digital age. All one needs to do, really, is recall the effect on this nation of a thirty-second clip of Los Angeles police officers beating an unarmed black motorist, and then consider the potential of a technology capable of splicing in a glimpse of a weapon or making the beating even more savage.

High-tech forgeries, like the lies they are, are easier offered than retracted; Pandora's box springs open at a touch – closing it is another matter. What is to prevent image-manipulation techniques – their usefulness already established in entertainment and advertising – from crossing the line (if there still is one) into political image making? What's to prevent the folks who can digitally slim Paulina's hips to please a client from using the same technology to make the candidate's eyes a deeper blue? Or to firm the jaw, straighten the posture, or adjust the carriage of the head? Not a thing. Production company presidents are already impressing prospective clients by demonstrating, for example, that Mario Cuomo can be made to seem as tall as Bill Bradley, and that Bill Clinton can be made to look drunk. Do they know what they're doing? Of course not. 'We're still in the horse and carriage days with this,' says the director Robert Zemeckis, whose film *Forrest Gump* uses computer-generated images to startling effect. 'We have no idea what impact this will have on the world. We couldn't imagine it if we tried.'[21]

But of course we can. Lies, if propagated in sufficient

quantity and repeated often enough, will generate their own truth, as Adolf Hitler explained. And so they have with us. So accustomed to illusions have we become that we seem increasingly ready to believe in them – as do the owners of digital fish – even when we know them to be false. Though aware, for example, of the inherently manipulative power of advertising, or the extent to which so-called reality-based television programs are rigged, we nonetheless seem willing to buy the products (and the realities) they sell. Though aware that the photo-op of the candidate washing dishes at a homeless shelter or gazing admiringly at a redwood is staged – even directly contrary to his or her actual policies – we vote as though the images actually had some bearing on reality.

What this suggests, if nothing else, is the enormous and abiding power of the visual sense; more than any other, it compels our faith. We want and need to believe what we see. The problem with this is that our instinctive allegiance to the things our eyes show us has been transferred, largely if not entirely, to images of things as well. We believe the photograph or the video image nearly as much as we do the original.

While this is hardly new – by 1961, Daniel Boorstin was complaining that 'the language of images is everywhere' and that 'the right "image" will elect a President or sell an automobile, a religion, a cigarette, or a suit of clothes'[22] – the *degree* to which it has become true today is something else again. Like customers at the checkout counter who find themselves staring at their own image in the ceiling video monitor, our collective attention, increasingly, seems to be Elsewhere.

It's easy to understand why. Every passing year, more and more of the things our eyes show us are facsimiles. Every year, the time most of us spend actually *seeing* our world – actual men's and women's bodies rather than models in advertisements, actual landscapes rather than images of landscapes on television – grows smaller. As technoevangelist Kevin Kelly has pointed out, 'we post-modern urbanites spend a huge portion of our day immersed in hyperrealities: phone conversations, TV viewing, computer screens, radio worlds. We value them highly.' An exaggeration? 'Try having a dinner conversation,' he suggests, 'without referencing something you saw or heard via the media!' His conclusion seems hard to argue with: 'Simulacra,' he claims, 'have become the terrain we live in. In more ways than we care to measure, the hyperreal is real for us.'[23]

All of which puts both digital fish and Rocky's appearance at Yalta in a new light: if, in fact, we are in the process of transferring our affections to a surrogate world, if simulacra are becoming, as Kelly claims, 'the terrain we live in,' then image-manipulation techniques carry the threat of manipulating not only the images we consume, but the very world we inhabit. They threaten, in other words, to make our world virtual to an extent unimaginable outside science fiction.

So why wasn't this a problem earlier? Because our willingness to believe in copies was kept in check by the inability of our technology to lie convincingly; though representations could be distorted or manipulated in various ways, out-and-out fabrications were either difficult to accomplish or readily detectable. Digital image manipulation has made lying easy. What does this mean? It means, as Ellen Hume, senior fellow at the Annenberg Washington Program, a media research center, has pointed out, that 'as the technology to alter video and still pictures becomes more widely available . . . photographic images that are now largely trusted as accurate are likely to be regarded as suspect.'[24] What the illusion business risks, in other words, is a wholesale crisis of faith, a crash in the reality market.

By flooding the culture with digitally manipulated images, I'm saying, we risk devaluing *all* visual representations and, by extension, the reality they pretend to depict. Which is no small thing. Allowed to run unchecked, the crisis I am describing could come to have a profound effect on Western democratic culture. How? By knocking out one of the supporting girders of the liberal democratic state: the belief in universal access to reliable information and therefore, by implication, to truth. I stress our *faith* in reliable information, rather than the fact, for the obvious reason that we have never achieved this ideal; despite the First Amendment and the Freedom of Information Act, information is neither universally available *nor* always dependable. And yet, in spite of this, our faith has remained largely intact. We believe. We believe that by and large, we are being told the facts, or that the facts are available to those of us willing to make an effort. Apply enough elbow grease, we assume, and the facts will appear like the grain of wood under layers of varnish.

Is this naive? Of course it is. But I'm not interested in rehashing the subject of Americans' political naïveté – that's been done before, and well. I'm interested, rather, in affirming its importance. Our credulousness, after all, like any faith too closely held, contains a threat; its loss, should it come too quickly, would be potentially devastating. Traditionally, the greatest apostates have come from the ranks of the most devout; here, too, we could expect the depth of our fall to be in direct proportion to the sublimity of our faith.

Which brings us to the danger posed by the technologies

of illusion. Simply put, our willingness to believe in the information made available to us is relatively harmless – even a strength in some respects – only as long as the information presented is, by and large, truthful. When it no longer is, our faith becomes the anchor that drags us down. What we risk *then* is nothing less than the kind of institutionalized cynicism found under authoritarian regimes.

At first blush, that may seem an unreasonable conclusion. I don't believe it is. In the former Eastern bloc, for example, the sort of blurring of fiction and reality that digital image manipulation would make even more complete was systemic. And this blurring, in turn, spawned a culturewide and pervasive cynicism toward all official information. A newspaper article or television news broadcast was automatically assumed to be a lie in direct proportion to its relevance for people's lives. The three-page spread on fertilizer techniques for the local farming cooperative? Probably true. The report on the state of the economy? Undoubtedly false.

The threat inherent in image-manipulation techniques is the threat of authoritarianism, of information control. Control the images the public consumes (alter them to suit a predetermined agenda) and Jefferson's notion of an informed populace, already threatened, goes right out the window. And exposing the frauds, I suspect, even if it becomes possible, will be of little help; once the public's faith in images is shaken, cynicism will spread like a contagion to *all* sources of information.

It is on this level, I think, that the photograph of Rocky at Yalta is so eloquent – and so ominous. It reminds us, or ought to, of the photograph that opens Milan Kundera's parable of authoritarianism, *The Book of Laughter and Forgetting*. In February 1948, Kundera writes, at the beginning of the Communist era in Czechoslovakia, the Communist leader, Klement Gottwald, stood on a balcony to give a speech to the people gathered below. It was cold. A comrade, a man named Klementis, lent Gottwald his hat. Pictures were taken. Four years later, Klementis was hanged for treason and promptly erased from all official photographs. Only his hat, forgotten by the censors, remained, still on Gottwald's head.

The photograph of Gottwald wearing Klementis's ghostly hat, we should realize, is an example of image manipulation, symbolic of the propaganda so prevalent under authoritarian regimes. Besides being considerably less amusing, how different is it from the photograph of Rocky at Yalta? Not much, really. Except for one thing: the photograph of Stallone and Co. is better; more accomplished, more technically sophisticated – in a word, more believable. As a forgery, despite its jokey content, it's light-years ahead of its crude Communist rival. Clearly, in the department of visual propaganda (as in so many other things), the unconstrained powers of the free market have been victorious. We now have the demonstrable, technical ability to lie better than they ever did, to show Churchill embracing Eichmann, or the Dalai Lama in Beijing. We can rearrange history (for what are visual images but historical records?) to suit our needs.[25]

In 1992, following the collapse of the Soviet Union, a State Department official named Francis Fukuyama rode to his fifteen minutes of fame on a much-discussed and quickly forgotten paean to the triumph of Western capitalism titled 'The End of History.' Fukuyama's essay and the book that emerged from it were quickly buried beneath the flood of events that devastated his sunny vision of a universal, free-market utopia. Perhaps they should be disinterred. If nothing else, the title could be clipped and pasted under the photograph of Rocky at Yalta, a fitting postscript. 'The End of History,' indeed.

Simulations, of course, come in all sizes. At Splendid China, a new Chinese-history theme park in Kissimmee, Florida, you can take the kids to see a perfect miniature replica of the Potala Palace of the Dalai Lama. They'll learn that for millions of Buddhists, the *real* Potala Palace is regarded as the world's most sacred place. What they *won't* learn about (you'll have to fill in) is China's 1959 invasion of Tibet, its ongoing genocide against the Tibetan peoples, or the fact that the real Potala Palace was closed as a religious center by the Chinese government and is now open only to tourists.

If virtual Tibetan history doesn't grab you, you'll soon be able to 'do' American history (in nine easy pieces) by visiting Disney's America, a proposed theme park currently in search of a home after being denied the right to desecrate the Manassas National Battlefield in Haymarket, Virginia.

What will Disney's America have to offer? Nearly everything, it seems. 'Real' audioanimatronic presidents who give speeches and debate one another; computer-simulation games designed to enable children to fly World War II bombing runs; a 'real' family farm, complete with real chickens and real cows capable of laying (one assumes) real eggs and giving real milk. You'll be able to visit an authentically recreated Indian village, complete with a Lewis and Clark whitewater ride, to play a Civil War soldier, or to 'feel what slavery was like.' 'Our goal,' says Peter Rummel (head of Disney Design and Development), 'is to make this real.'[26] One could argue, of course, that seeing Dad bayonetted on the battlefield, being separated from one's family, or getting bullwhipped might make the experience even *more* realistic. But reality, to be profitable, must have its limits. At Disney's America, the Civil War dead with the ketchup on their breasts will be resurrected every afternoon at closing time, and the slave on the auction block, newly emancipated, will pass you on the highway as he hurries home for dinner.

The 'theming of America,' as Ada Louise Huxtable points out, is not limited to tourist enterprises like Disney's America. In our towns and along our highways, frontier facades hide four-star restaurants, real! live! authentic! simulations line the way west, and faux Main Streets appear inside suburban shopping malls even as real Main Streets, effectively malled, die across the nation.[27]

The general breakdown of the barrier separating original from simulation, fact from fake, is visible everywhere; the slow bleeding of reality into illusion is systemic. The image of O. J. Simpson dodging tackles or hurdling luggage en route to his Hertz rent-a-car blurs with the newspaper and TV images of O. J. on the lam, O. J. clowning with Leslie Neilsen, O. J. and Alan Dershowitz (or is it Ron Silver?) hurdling legal landmines on the way to a possible acquittal and *Reversal of Fortune II*. The horrific videotape of the Rodney King beating (repeated ad nauseum or, worse, until it became inseparable from any other made-for-TV beating) blurs with the image of Rodney King uttering the made-for-TV sound byte, 'can't we all just get along?' which in turn blurs with images of rioting in south central L.A., which look just like the 'real-life' scenes of Los Angeles mayhem found on Police Quest: Open Season, a video game designed by none other than former Los Angeles police chief Daryl Gates. The furniture swims, the walls bulge and bend; simulacra, as technoevangelist Kevin Kelly might say, are the order of the day.

Is any part of the culture exempt from the assault of

virtual realities? Apparently not. In American courts of law, professionally rendered re-enactments are becoming increasingly popular (in injury-compensation cases, for example) and are admissible as evidence. Juries, made up of individuals weaned, like the rest of us, on simulations, find them very effective. The re-enactments are scripted, rehearsed, directed, and edited. Nothing is too extreme. Was your hand crushed at the factory? Were your kids burned to death in a car accident? For a hefty fee, a company will provide a video simulation complete with realistic screams, horrified bystanders, and virtual blood. Think of it as reality-based television for the courtroom. Or the tenth segment of Disney's America: 'The Legal Experience.'

What does the judicial system's willingness to admit re-enactments as evidence have to do with Disney's America, or with Rocky at Yalta, or with digital fish, for that matter? Simply this: it is both a symptom of and a contributing cause to the erosion of reality in our culture. All four, after all – the virtual accident, the virtual slave auction, the virtual photograph, and the virtual guppie – are re-enactments, representative of an increasingly virtual world in which, to recall Michael Kelly for a moment, the boundary between reality and fantasy is becoming more and more porous. As the virtually real becomes good enough, the dividing line between what is and what appears to be, what was and what might have been, will be lost.

At that point, the already slippery distinction between our America and Disney's will disappear for good, the re-enactment will triumph over the original event, and the culture of illusion – announced by the president 'playing' an 'imitation' of himself on Saturday Night Live, as ex-President George Bush did, not too long ago – will have arrived. Just in time for the millennium.

CHAPTER 6

The Case for Essentialism

Let me start my conclusion with a familiar bit of free-market heresy: what's good for business is not necessarily good for culture. The digital revolution is probably good business;[1] culturally, in many ways, it's bad news.

It's bad news – another, larger heresy – at least in part because it's a product of the new globalism; and globalism, while both admirable as a metaphor for tolerance and effective as a marketing strategy, is an abstraction at once too vast and too airy for most people to live by.[2] Human beings, no less than other species, are more local than global. We are shaped, each of us, by the particulars of the cultures we inhabit. Identity, in other words, is in the details, and though the individual may color these details in his or her own way, the physical aspect of life in the real world is an invaluable source of self-knowledge.

It's a kind of self-knowledge directly threatened by the abstractions of the digital revolution, whose backers, like former Citicorp chairman Walter B. Wriston and current U.S. Secretary of Labor Robert Reich, laud the I-Way's ability to 'empower' individuals, without bothering to point out that empowerment has more than one definition. What they offer us, generally speaking, is a vision of cyberspace as free-market utopia; what they tend to leave out is any suggestion that abstracting our lives may be bad for us, that the virtual community – to use the title of Howard Rheingold's book – is an oxymoron, and that the new global citizen may actually turn out to be a new kind of exile – an electronic wanderer wired to the world but separated from much that matters in human life.[3] Cyberspace may be 'where your money is,' as the computer visionary Chip Morningstar so neatly put it, but it may not be where *you* want to be.

Why not? Because, to recall Gertrude Stein, there's no there there. Because cyberspace, quite literally, is nowhere – an electronic space that mimics the forms of social life even as it confirms us in our isolation. Old men don't play horseshoes in cyberspace communities. Teenagers don't make out under the bleachers. Kids can't catch frogs or play stickball or jump in leaf piles. We can't see each other smile or pass a bottle of wine. And typing the words 'I kiss your lips in the barred dark of the bleachers,' or 'I jump out of the low branches into the leaf pile,' or 'I clink my glass to yours as the music plays from the back room,' isn't quite the same as doing these things, no matter how strenuously the technoevangelists may argue that it is.

Some will say, of course, that my examples are something out of Norman Rockwell, that the life I see missing from cyberspace communities is already long gone, that today, old men die alone in retirement communities, that the only activity done beneath the bleachers is apt to be conducted at knifepoint, and that all the frogs are dead or dying. But even if this were so – and I don't believe, generally speaking, that it is – it would still leave us with only one option: to reclaim the territory we have lost. To rebuild our shattered communities, to revive our capacity for F2F (face-to-face) communication, to restore the denatured wastelands too many of us are forced to call home.[4]

The Case for Essentialism

Distracting ourselves from the realities of late-twentieth-century life is clearly not the answer. And yet that, in a nutshell, is what the digital revolution offers us: distraction on a grand scale – the option of turning our attention Elsewhere, to an abstract, more easily manipulable world. It's a world that, seen from the right angle, is lacking just about everything, and yet millions, increasingly disgusted, frustrated, or bored with *this* world, already accustomed – like the good children of the television age they are – to accepting representations in place of the real thing, are checking into it. As this culture of distraction comes to play an increasingly significant role in American life, it will become more and more necessary to refocus our attention on *actual* communities, on *real* friends and neighbors, on the significance and value of our *physical* rather than our virtual environments. These, after all, are sources of information too – a slow, subtle, ultimately invaluable kind of information, irreducible to binary code.

It may be that *this* kind of information, the kind that comes from experience in the physical world, is the kind we are least capable of doing without. As researchers in a wide variety of disciplines are beginning to show, we remain genetically 'wired' to the physical world in profound and unalterable ways. Having evolved over hundreds of thousands of generations in response to the constraints and pressures of the natural world, we are, quite literally, its products, dependent upon it for our psychological and physical well-being and even, some argue, for our very identity as social creatures.

The best argument against the abstract communities and virtual landscapes of the digital age, therefore, may be biological. The brain, as the Nobel Prize-winning biologist E. O. Wilson has pointed out, 'evolved in a biocentric world, not a machine-regulated world'; to assume that we can sever our connection to the physical environment in which the mind originated, and in which it remains 'permanently rooted,' therefore, is foolish. 'Evolution,' says Robert Park, professor of physics at the University of Maryland, 'is a very slow business. It cannot keep up with the pace of change in recent decades.' Trapped in an increasingly alien world, a world more and more at odds with our biological selves, 'the wonder is not that some of us act strangely at times or hold irrational beliefs but that we cope at all.'[5]

Wilson's and Park's point is simple: while our relationship to time and space and distance has been fundamentally altered by technology, we have remained the same; we don't run any faster, see any better, meet or mate or eat much differently than we did half a million years ago. What this suggests is a growing gap between our biological selves – rooted in physical reality – and the increasingly rapid, synthetic world we inhabit. As technological developments carry us ever more rapidly into the virtual future, we risk tearing ourselves loose from our own biological past – the basis, in the deepest sense, of all we know and are.[6]

This notion of a deeper, biological self, while easily parodied as some New Age fad, is gathering support from members of the scientific community. In *The Power of Place*, for example, Winifred Gallagher has argued that human beings are genetically encoded to respond to their environment in certain ways that haven't changed over millennia. We respond favorably to natural vistas – to forests and rivers and lakes – because for thousands of generations, nature was our home. Take away all vestiges of the natural, and a host of neuroses begin to appear. 'If we complete the destruction of nature,' writes Dr. David W. Orr of Oberlin College, 'we will have succeeded in cutting ourselves off from the source of sanity itself. Hermetically sealed amidst our creations . . . the world will then reflect only the demented image of the mind imprisoned within itself.'[7]

Slowly but steadily, the evidence is coming in to support Orr's thesis: one ten-year study of patients recovering from gallbladder surgery, for example, showed that patients able to look out on trees and sky had significantly shorter hospital stays and took fewer painkillers than those deprived of these views. In another study, a clinic providing Alzheimer's patients with access to specially designed gardens recorded a dramatic decrease in panic attacks and violent incidents.[8]

If we expand the definition of *environment* to include the human community as well, the implications of sealing ourselves off amid our creations – which is precisely what the digital revolution threatens to do – become doubly ominous. An evening spent with friends, researchers are showing, can measurably enhance the immune system for two days; cancer support groups that actually meet in real life can double the survival time of their participants. Social life, in other words, whatever its strains and difficulties, is a life-enhancing thing. Isolation and stress, on the other hand, demonstrably take their toll.[9]

Both isolation *and* stress, however, are direct by-products of the digital world, a world, as the author Brent Staples has noted, increasingly 'devoid of quiet and empty spaces, where every surface shouts and every silence is filled.'[10] Wired together, permanently in touch, we're both more alone than ever and, paradoxically perhaps, never at peace.

On the one hand, like those baseball fans who already bring portable radios and televisions to the ballpark, we're increasingly isolated from the person next to us – a trend that is likely to continue, by the way, as Major League clubs install computers in stadium seats to allow fans to 'access' statistics, view graphs, and even play sports trivia games during the game.[11] Instead of appreciating the batter's stroke, or talking to our neighbor between innings, we're off in virtual reality. And the same isolating trend that's visible in the ballpark is visible elsewhere as well: instead of walking the message down the hall to a real person, we're sending E-mail; instead of talking to our companion at dinner, we're staring at the TV over the bar; instead of sitting on the stoop or going to the local pub or coffeehouse, we're socializing in cyberspace or watching representations of actors socialize on television.

On the other hand, *despite* our growing isolation, the push for complete 'in-touchedness,' Staples argues, 'offers a glimpse at the end of solitude, of a time . . . when portable phones, pagers and data transmission devices of every sort keep us terminally in touch, permanently patched into the grid.' Deprived of unstructured moments and precious time off, we'll lose the opportunity to nourish 'what is valuable in us,' to gain insight into how we live and what we believe. Solitude, he suggests – and I'm inclined to agree – will become "down time," to be filled in with gadgets.'[12]

Though it hardly needs saying, neither our growing isolation from the world around us nor the disappearance of solitude from our lives is of any concern to the gurus of the New Age, who maintain that the cure for whatever ails us is always and forever more information. 'People are frightened by the thought of getting too much information,' the Nobel laureate Arno Penzias complained to the science writer James Gleick recently, adding: 'Are you frightened by the thought of getting too much money? Too much happiness?'[13]

Penzias's equation – information = money = happiness –

suggests something of both the cyberists' infatuation with the very idea of information as well as their attitude toward limits in general: for these people, much is good; more is always better. It should come as no surprise that many, both within and outside the scientific community, remain unconvinced. In our rush to wire ourselves up, cultural critics like Neil Postman are pointing out, we're forgetting that 'there are very few political, social, and especially personal problems that arise because of insufficient information' and quite a few that arise as a result of mindlessly equating human progress with the sheer tonnage of information we are able to receive.[14]

Does information equal happiness? Does bandwidth compensate for the world? More telling than the words of skeptics like Postman (and myself) are the actions of some of the digerati themselves, whose private lives quite often belie their own rhetoric. Currently, for example, there's a full-fledged 'back-to-the-land' movement taking place among high-tech Silicon Valley executives; rapidly buying up land in bucolic Napa Valley, the digerati, it seems, are planting grapevines, tending them with care, then sharing the fruits of their labor with their neighbors. Why aren't they planting in cyberspace? Why are they reaching out to real neighbors when digital ones are just as good? Why does even Bill Gates's 40,000-square-foot, high-tech Xanadu in the making contain an estuary and a salmon stream?

'When you're in high-tech,' says F. H. Hyler, owner of Logical Marketing Inc. of Menlo Park, 'every once in a while you just want to . . . get closer to humanity.' And nature, apparently. The value, Hyler points out, 'is in the quality of life, the openness and honesty.' Which is precisely the point, after all. What suffers on the Net, as even some of the converted seem to realize, is the quality of our lives. As Mr. Gates's architects allegedly argued, transparent,

three-dimensional virtual reality rooms would only go
so far. The Gates's children might one day want to see
'something no more complicated than ducks on a pond or
a fish in a stream.'[15]

Shifting our attention from the digital abstractions that
surround us to the physical world we inhabit will require,
above all, cultivating a certain skepticism toward the
pronouncements of the technologically enraptured. Which
won't be easy. Relentlessly high-pitched, unflaggingly
enthusiastic, the technoevangelists are often both hard
to ignore and very convincing. So confident do they seem
that one assumes there must be something to their vision.
Quite often, there isn't. Quite often, in fact, the apparently
substantive argument, on closer inspection, turns out to be
as airy as cyberspace itself, one part speculation and two
parts wish-fulfillment fantasy.

Consider, for example, the uplifting predictions found
in George Gilder's *Life After Television: The Coming Transformation of Media and American Life*. Like other advocates of
'convergence,' who envision a future in which everything
is linked to just about everything else, Gilder believes
that the television, the computer, and the telephone are
coming together, and that the new hybrid birth, the
networked 'telecomputer,' will be an improvement all
around. 'Rather than exalting mass culture,' he writes,
'the telecomputer will enhance individualism. Rather than
cultivating passivity, the telecomputer will promote cre-
ativity . . . Perhaps most important, the telecomputer will
enrich and strengthen democracy and capitalism all around
the world.'[16]

Three years later, the wheat has separated from the
virtual chaff. What's left, as James Barron demonstrates
in a recent article for the *New York Times*, is an emerging
technology that combines the worst of television – its

126

addictiveness, its passivity – with the worst of on-line communication – its self-conscious glorification of superfice, its pop-culture chattiness, its pointless immediacy.[17] The result is a two-headed monster no less stupefying and, on the whole, no less insipid than the single-headed one it replaced. And potentially a whole lot more coercive.

What the coming together of computers and television has done, Barron shows, is vastly expand the power of the TV. Rather than doing *away* with the couch potato, the telecomputer has actually created a new, more tenacious variety of tuber: the individual who swivels from television screen to computer monitor without missing a beat, who logs on between commercials to talk about what he's just seen, then turns back to the TV when the show returns. For those 'hooked on the deadly combination of computers and TV,' Barron writes, 'when the closing credits roll on one, the show is just beginning on the other.' The result is an 'infoholic's wonderland,' in which a one-hour television show like *The X-Files* can generate hundreds of hours of on-line conversations a week.

Is Barron being mean-spirited? Not at all. Even the most casual stroll down the Infobahn confirms the range and power of the phenomenon he describes. Seemingly everywhere one looks in cyberspace, one finds chat groups (hundreds of them) crowded with individuals whose one interest, apparently, is television trivia; everywhere one turns there are bulletin board services choked with comments pouring in hourly from individuals dying to commune electronically with others like themselves about whether Darlene is really the bitch Jayna says she is, and whether she will or won't have Garret's baby. What's on in cyberspace? More often than not the answer is: the TV.

As a marketing strategy, of course, bringing television on-line makes sense. 'What network television does,' says

J. Ann Selzer, a partner in a communications firm in Des Moines, 'is to produce people for audiences to fall in love with. People who are in that stage of infatuation can't get enough information.' The on-line services, she explains, follow up on the need, providing photos, behind the scenes news, community chats, and so on, which together feed the 'love affair that the networks are doing their darnedest to create.'[18]

On-line services, in other words, allow you to enter the picture; their hook is the illusion of involvement. Instead of sitting passively by the tube, you can order press kits from the studios, upload pictures of the stars, criticize Brandon's new haircut on *Beverly Hills 90210*, or organize on-line baby showers for pregnant television actresses, as fans of *The X-Files* did recently for Gillian Anderson. In short, you can be part of the show.

It's a phenomenon as perversely fascinating as it is pathetic; like extras hoping to catch a glimpse of our own faces in the crowd, we're so entranced with our participation that we hardly care what it is we're participating in. 'The vast wasteland,' to recall Newton N. Minow's description of television, remains unchanged, but now our own chatter animates the stillness, even as TV writers, closing the circle, listen in quietly to our ghostly conversations in order to calibrate their next offerings to the national mood of the week.[19]

What all this suggests, of course, is that much if not all of the giddiness surrounding the digital revolution must be taken with a grain of salt. Instead of rousing the creative individual slumbering within, the union of the television and the computer has, in effect, opened a new kind of electronic theme park, a theme park in which we play the role of both admiring audience and admired object. Instead of strengthening democracy, as

Gilder predicted, the new technology has made it possible
– by refracting in a million conversations the 'information'
provided by the likes of *Married with Children* – for us to
spend our days talking to electronic companions about
the lives of electronic illusions. Instead of empowering
us, it has empowered the networks and their advertisers
by extending the culture of the tube and strengthening its
already enormous hold on our lives. 'This new technology
is riding us; we are not riding it,' says no less an authority
on virtual reality than Peggy Noonan, the author and
former speechwriter for President Ronald Reagan.[20] It's
a conclusion that's difficult to argue with.

If the hard facts contradict so dramatically the dreams of
the digerati, why then do we continue to listen to them?
Why do we, like gullible Easterners conned into buying
nonexistent land in Arizona, continue to invest in their new
*un*real estate in record numbers? Why, finally, if the new
technologies run contrary to the needs of human nature,
do we passively sit by as an entire generation of children
grows up in cyberspace? At least part of the explanation
may be due to the hype surrounding the digital revolution
almost from its inception, a hype based largely on the
time-tested notion of inevitability.

The new virtual technologies, my brother-in-law believes,
are inevitable. Cyberspace communities, the visionaries
inform me, are inevitable. Global-positioning wristwatches
– and electronic receptionists that can recognize a caller's
voice print and either accept a call or artfully dissemble
depending on who's on the line – are inevitable. The computer designer Carol Peters and the Hollywood producer
Jeff Apple have developed a computerized, interactive
television service for children, part Disneyland-style theme
park, part *Sesame Street*. Their company, Davinci Time

and Space, will provide 'a computerized space' in which children will be able to play games, watch videos, learn or simply hang out with other children with similar access to interactive cable systems.'[21] Ms. Peters thinks this kind of specialized service for kids is, you guessed it, inevitable.

Which is interesting, I think. Inevitability, after all, has not always been seen as a virtue. Until recently, the only inevitable things in life were death and taxes, a short list to which we now, apparently, must add digital books, virtual office parties, and the development of computerized playgrounds for our children. 'Kids are really accustomed to cyberspace,' claims Denise Caruso, editorial director of the Technology and Media Group, which publishes, not coincidentally, an industry newsletter. 'The whole notion of virtual community is something that adults marvel at,' she adds, 'but it's like breathing to kids.'[22]

That leaves most of us with two options. We can stand by and watch ourselves turn into veritable dinosaurs, out of touch with the world in which our own children (or so we are told) already frolic like so many happy guppies in a farm pond. Or we can buy a lot of very expensive stuff. Wondering (privately or publicly) whether cyberspace playgrounds are good or necessary – whether, in fact, they make sense at all – does not appear on the menu of options.

Why not? Because the aura of inevitability makes for good marketing strategy. It determines by fiat what might otherwise be open to discussion. It alters the playing field, changing the questions that might still be asked from whether to when, from Is it good? to How much will it cost me? Which may explain why no one seems to have considered the possibility that children take 'naturally' to cyberspace for the same reason they believe that elephants with large ears can fly – because children under the age of eight or so have a hard time separating illusion from reality – and why no one has pointed out that children's susceptibility to something is not necessarily a good indicator of its value, for adults *or* children. Kids take naturally to cyberspace? They take naturally to Barney, too. And they're cuckoo for Cocoa Puffs. So what?

Rarely in the history of this country has a new technology been sold as effectively; not since the advent of the television have such outrageous claims been made for one; never, to my knowledge, has one steamrollered so completely the voices of caution or dissent. We seem, as a culture, to have bought into the New Age lock, stock, and modem. We accept – it's almost an article of faith with us – that the information superhighway will make everything easier, faster, better; that it will make us (and our children) more knowledgeable, more imaginative, more creative;[23] that if we want to teach Jane or Johnny to read, ABC blocks and children's primers won't do: if we really want them to have a toe-in at Harvard Hall, they'll need a three-thousand-dollar computer with all the fixings. So hypnotized have we become, in fact, that we have to pinch ourselves to remember that literacy existed even before the invention of the microchip and that the imagination was doing quite well, thank you, long before the arrival of fiber-optic cable.

Among the true digerati, as one might expect, the tendency to credit the computer with just about everything reaches new and inspired heights. For the cyberspace theorist Nicole Stenger, for example, who teaches at the University of Washington in Seattle, spending time in cyberspace 'changes our sensitivity to light, to depth, makes our dreams more vivid, facilitates the use of metaphors in language . . . induces euphoria, [and] boosts intuition.' But 'this power of revelation and embodiment will be felt by many to be the utmost obscenity,' she warns. Why? Because 'freedom of imagination is feared by most powers,' and cyberspace is all about the freedom of the imagination. 'Let's not forget,' she concludes, ominously, 'that both Hitler and Stalin are known to have banned the publication of fairy tales.'[24] The slippery syllogism here goes something like this. Cyberspace is the domain of the imagination. Totalitarian regimes hate the imagination. Therefore, those who argue against cyberspace have totalitarian tendencies.

This is enough to make even reasonable individuals put down their books and prepare for battle against those goose-stepping haters of freedom and Little Red Riding Hood – the antitechnologists – no doubt already marching on the republic of the spirit. But wait! Does cyberspace have any particular relationship to either freedom or fairy tales? No. Does cyberspace facilitate 'the use of metaphors in language,' any more than writing a letter does? No. Does cyberspace, finally, have anything at all to do with the imagination? Why, yes, it does, but not in the way that Ms. Stenger says it does.

Nicole Stenger, in fact, has it backward. The real threat to the imagination comes *not* from some hidden cabal of anticomputer fanatics, but from people like herself: technophiles arrogant or foolish enough to try to convince us that a computer game is the last bastion of the imagination. What's truly authoritarian here, if we *must* look for bogeymen, is the attempt to argue that the survival of something as protean and vast as the imagination is dependent on the success of a technology – any technology – or to label as fascist anyone who suggests that our slide into virtual reality may not necessarily be a good thing, particularly for the young.[25]

To anchor all this, consider a recent IBM computer

advertisement in *The New Yorker*. From a blank white page, a beautiful eight-year-old in pigtails and overalls looks up at the reader. Above her head, in a narrow black band at the top of the page, are the words: 'Ellie Frame could view the Mona Lisa, the Grand Canyon, the statue of David, the Great Wall of China – and be back in time for The Fresh Prince of Bel-Air – if she had a PS/1 with built in CD-ROM.' Just below these words is a miniature rendering of the PS/1, showing a picture of some medieval edifice on its color screen. It looks unthreatening, user-friendly – like a TV with a keyboard.

What's wrong with this picture? For one thing, it recalls the infoholic's wonderland described by James Barron. For Ellie Frame, when one program ends, the other is just beginning. (In fact, if she has a Compaq Presario, a computer and TV in one, she won't even have to switch screens.) For another, it suggests that the only way Ellie can see these wonders is if Mom and Dad sock a PS/1 on the Visa card, neatly ignoring the fact that even the most budgetarily challenged lending library in the country will offer a dozen books on each subject for free.[26] Finally, what the ad fails to point out is that as Ellie moves from one screen to the next, as the statue of David blurs into the Fresh Prince of Bel-Air, the distinction between the two is necessarily weakened. The Mona Lisa and the Grand Canyon become, in effect, another show; the world is reduced to the lowest common denominator of the television sitcom.[27]

What the computer folk don't want to talk about, understandably, is the flattening effect the world of computer representations – or any other electronic representations – can have on the individual imagination. The imagination, as the novelist Sven Birkerts has argued, eloquently and persuasively, requires room to move.[28] In the spaces and silences of a text or, better yet, in its contacts with the physical world, the imagination can roam at will, can create and flourish. In the claustrophobic, overdetermined world of a television show (or a computer program), there's no wiggle space. Everything is provided. It comes down to this: the most sophisticated computer program can never offer the range of 'options' available, free of charge, to the individual imagination, can never match the sheer wonder of a faculty capable of turning a pencil into a harpoon or a tabletop into a three-masted schooner. What it *can* do, as Douglas Sloan, professor of the history of education at Columbia University's Teacher's College has pointed out, is cramp and limit the imagination, force it to walk along certain paths and not others, reduce it, basically – and us along with it – to a function of technology.[29]

My gripe with the digital revolution, to put it bluntly, is that it offers too little and demands too much. What it offers is information, lots and lots of information, and a new, abstract kind of 'connectedness.' What it asks in return is that we shift our allegiance from the physical world to the virtual one. It's a bad deal – not just because it ignores our biological needs, but because it limits our autonomy.

Unmediated reality, after all, is a profoundly democratic thing; we experience the world, each of us, in subtly different ways, and this diversity is both the foundation of our independence and a bulwark against authoritarianism. Representations, on the other hand – particularly the mass-produced, electronic kind – limit diversity. However great the range of 'personal options' they afford, they are a homogenizing force; they turn us, in other words, from individuals into an audience. And this is a dangerous thing. Not only does it raise the specter of manipulation – the more homogeneous the group, the easier it is to manipulate – but it suggests that at some point we ourselves, increasingly unaccustomed to the rigors of individual judgment, may come to mistake mass opinion for our own.

This, it seems to me, is the threat we face: that soon, lost among electronic representations 'just as good' as the real thing, we'll collectively lose sight of the fact that approximations and re-enactments are a kind of lie, and that lies, even small ones, tend to create a climate increasingly hostile or indifferent to truth. We'll forget, in other words, that the virtual head of a company is not the head; that virtually dead means alive; that something virtually true or virtually real is false. As the percentage of reality coming to us prepackaged or second hand continues to rise, we'll grow increasingly frightened of unmediated reality; more and more isolated, we'll come to depend, first for our comfort and eventually for our very sanity, on the technologies and the people behind them who offer to stand between us and the hostile world we inhabit, who offer us the platitudes, fictions, and out-and-out lies on which we've come to depend, who shield us from the increasingly terrifying aura of first-hand experience.

How can we begin making our way back from the virtual brink? *Not*, it seems to me, by reasserting some simpleminded or unitary truth – the preferred solution of right-wing zealots nationwide – nor by instituting, say, some secular version of the Islamic injunction against representations in general, but by resuscitating our faith in truth in general, by recognizing its importance, by rededicating ourselves to its pursuit.[30] And how do we do *that*? By returning, whenever possible, to original things; by recognizing that truth, and a respect for truth, are somehow linked to a respect for reality, and that respect for reality depends on a life lived close to the physical world. What we need, in other words, is a revolution, in sensibility as well as in lifestyle, capable of freeing us from our overdependence on abstractions; a revolution capable of reconnecting us to essential things – the things, that is, that we can experience directly and for ourselves, not through the mediating influence of technology.

What essentialism suggests – and this is important – is nothing radical. Nothing new. What it advocates is not the *creation* of some brave new world, but the *rejection* of one through small, incremental gestures, gestures as apparently insignificant as turning off the television now and then. Or going for a walk with a friend. Or spending the morning lying in a hammock. Or getting personally involved in some community issue. Or stressing face-to-face meetings over inter-office memoranda.

The incentive? Not utopia, certainly, nor paradise regained, but quite conceivably something like the sense of psychological well-being that one gets from coming clean after having become entangled in a net of lies and half-truths. What we stand to gain, in other words, is nothing less than a right relation to the world, a renewed sense of clarity in our lives. We'll know – or at least have a better chance of knowing – where we belong, who we are (and are not), and what our priorities should be. And thus empowered, we'll be better able to recognize and rebuff the more sophisticated kinds of propaganda the blurmeisters pass our way.

There are some positive signs. In the fields of architecture and community planning, to take just one example, the trend is clearly away from the atomized, single-family home separated from areas of recreation, work, and commerce. From Swedish and Belgian experiments in cooperative and semicommunal living to Florida's 'Seaside' community, planners are responding to a growing demand for change, for a return to communities in which shops and schools and parks are all walking distance, in which the physical layout encourages, rather than discourages, physical communication between neighbors. Shopping malls are being replaced by Main Streets. Driveways are being moved to back alleys. Front porches and wide sidewalks are making a comeback.

'Man's development,' wrote the drama critic and naturalist Joseph Wood Krutch in 1949, 'takes him farther and farther away from his associations with his fellows, seems to condemn him more and more to live with what is dead rather than what is alive.'[31] A small but growing segment of the population seems unwilling to accept that. Neither antiscience fanatics nor neo-Luddites nor New Age Puritans, these individuals, many of them respected members of the scientific community, are simply asking that progress – long associated with the ideas and technologies that distance us from both the landscape and one another – be realigned with human needs.[32] They're taking another look at the machines being sold to us and asking which are good or useful, and which aren't, which improve our lives, individually and culturally, and which do not. And more and more, they're finding that the machines that are good for us are those that do not try to substitute for the social or natural world or rob us of our self-sufficiency.

The skeptics, of course, are a tiny minority, and, at least for the moment, there's no reason to expect them to become anything more. The momentum of the digital revolution, after all, is formidable; the financial incentive it represents for its advocates, enormous; our own familiarity with illusions, not least, well-established. History itself, finally, is less than encouraging. Nearly fifty years ago, E. B. White predicted our course with eerie accuracy. His prophecy, which we seem determined to fulfil, serves equally well as both warning to the unaware and incentive to the as yet unwired.

In the not-so-distant future, White wrote, our technologies 'will insist that we forget the primary and the near in favor of the secondary and the remote.' As we grow used to 'digesting ideas, sounds, images – distant and concocted, . . . a door closing, heard over the air; a face contorted, seen in a panel of light – these will emerge as the real and the true; and when we bang the door of our own cell or look into another's face, the impression will be of mere artifice.' I see a time, White concluded, 'when the solid world becomes make-believe . . . when all is reversed and we shall be like the insane, to whom the antics of the sane seem the crazy twistings of a grig.'[33]

That time, without waxing apocalyptic, may be sooner than we think. Some are already residents in White's asylum; the rest of us stand at the door. Whether we enter or choose to remain in the real world is ultimately up to us, no one else.

Glossary

'Cyberspace,' writes Meredith Bricken, a research scientist at the Human Interface Technology Laboratory at the University of Washington, 'is still in its definitional infancy. The lexicon is in formative turbulence, and the relationship of existing information technology to virtual world implementations is not entirely clear.' Indeed. Virtual reality, in other words, seems to have engendered its own virtual language, a hash of verbal nouns, polysyllabic acronyms, strange mutations born of poststructuralist jargon and pop culture, information theory and infotainment. I've done my best to avoid them all. For those few instances when I've failed, the following – a bare-bones, highly subjective guide to techno-rap for the unwired and the unhived – may be of some use.

avatar: the persona one adopts in cyberspace; one's virtual stand-in or alter ego. When Bob logs on, he assigns himself a name. He can call himself Bob, or make himself into whoever or whatever he wants to be: human, animal, vegetable, or mineral; Marlene Dietrich or a talking yam. (See *gender surfing*.)

bandwidth: the amount of information exchanged in a unit of time. Reality, as cyberspace theorists are fond of pointing out, is wide-bandwidth, because when people meet face to face, the amount of information carried through personal expressions, gestures, and speech is immense. Computer network conversations, by contrast, are narrow-bandwidth, because communication is limited to a line of text on a screen. The goal of many of those involved in cyberspace research today is to widen the bandwidth of communications technologies to a level approximating or equaling reality.

bulletin board service (BBS): generally a small (though not always), noncommercial service devoted to a specialty issue or topic. By logging on to a BBS, one can talk to likeminded others, download information, play games, and so on.

cyberism: the drive to animate or personalize our environment by making it more responsive to our needs and wishes through the use of smart technology – for example, new, 'sensitive' furniture containing microchips that can identify a user and adjust accordingly to suit that person's contours, weight, and so on.

cybersex: masturbating while sharing a fantasy on a computer Net with someone else logged on at the same time. Generally speaking, two individuals pretending to be anyone or anything they want, describe a sexual encounter between themselves. Phone sex without the voice. Also known as Netsex, tinysex, virtual sex, and, (my personal favorite) teledildonics.

cyberspace: not a space in the standard, three-dimensional sense of the word, but a metaphor, a symbolic 'place' we 'inhabit' but are not present in physically. The telephone is an obvious, if primitive, example. When we make a telephone call we, and the party on the other end, meet in a sort of symbolic space. We communicate – share information, emotions, and so on – yet are not physically present. Cyberspace is also sometimes referred to as the Net.

cyborg: machine-human hybrid.

cyborgasm: something one receives from (or gives to, presumably) a cyborg. A big deal for those busy pondering the future of cybersex. When fully sensual virtual reality becomes a reality (if one can put it that way), cyborgasms will be all the rage.

digital image manipulation: see *image manipulation.*

download: to bring something from cyberspace (a document, a photograph, or whatever else can travel over the wires) down to one's own computer, where, if one chooses, it can be printed out in hard copy.

flame: violent attack (verbal, of course) on another person in cyberspace.

flame war: a continuous round of flames between warring parties.

gender surfing: adopting a different gender in cyberspace by giving oneself a name that implies a different gender from one's own. Most gender surfing, according to the experts, is male to female. For some reason, adolescent males on the Net seem to have a great desire to play the roles of hypersexed females. One of the pastimes on the Net, therefore, is *outing*: exposing someone's real gender by seeing through their persona.

hyper-: same as *cyber*. As far as I have been able to discover, the sole purpose of this prefix is to confuse the uninitiated.

image manipulation: a catch-all term for a variety of computer-based, image-altering techniques; a kind of forgery involving visual images. Basically, it works like this: a special camera breaks up a black-and-white or color print into microscopic units called cells, or pixels, each of which – its color saturation, hue, and intensity – is then recorded on disk. The pixels are then moved around, or replaced altogether, to alter the original picture. When one image is altered to change fluidly into an entirely different one – on a videotape, for example – it's called *morphing*.

Infobahn: see *information superhighway*.

Information superhighway: also known as the I-Way, the Info-way, the Infobahn, the global communications network, and so on. Basically refers to the total mass of computers interlinked around the world, through which flows the 'traffic' of information. Also referred to as the Net.

Info-way: see *information superhighway*.

Internet: the mother of all networks. A collection of thousands of computer networks connected to one another by a common computer language. Not all smaller networks are connected to the Internet, though they probably will be in the relatively near future.

I-Way: see *information superhighway.*

modem: a machine that hooks up the computer to the phone lines and allows one to communicate with other computers, download information, and so on.

MOO: Multiple User Dungeons, Object-Oriented. A MUD (which see) that is object-oriented. The object will be an imaginary place – often described in amazing detail – that one can enter by calling up and setting up a role. The difference between a MOO and a MUD, generally speaking, is that the MOO allows the individual user to create his or her own space – to add on to the virtual world by describing virtual rooms, furniture, hallways, and so on. The MUDs, by contrast, are more fixed in their dimensions.

morphing: see *image manipulation.*

MUD: Multiple User Dimension or Multiple User Dungeon. Same as a MUSH and a MOO. For the moment, the more common term.

MUSH: Multiple User Shared Hallucination. For all practical purposes, a MUSH is a MUD is a MOO. Basically a computer game in which one can take on a role, maneuver around a virtual world – a town, say, or a system of caves – and interact with other people who have taken on roles.

Net: refers to the millions of computers linked, or networked, worldwide. Also referred to as cyberspace. Also referred to, by Al Gore and others, as the information highway, information superhighway, I-Way, Infobahn, and so on and so on. The Net, however, seems to be used more often by the purists – the true cybernauts. For these folk, the Net is a quasi-mystical term not necessarily referring to the Internet (which see), but rather, as John Perry Barlow puts it, to 'the great cloud of words, images, and sounds that floats above all the [computer codes] on all the hard disks of all the connected computers in the world.'

Netsex: see *cybersex.*

PONA: Person of No Account. Anyone who does not have an account in cyberspace, that is, anyone not on-line. If you don't know what a modem is, you're a PONA.

teledildonics: see *cybersex.*

tinysex: see *cybersex.*

upload: to send something (a document, for example) from one's own computer into cyberspace. Cyberists such as John Perry Barlow, expanding on the term, talk of human beings uploading themselves into the Net, that is, transferring their lives from the physical world into cyberspace.

virtual reality: also known as augmented reality and synthetic space. A very slippery term, fittingly enough, often used interchangeably with *cyberspace.* More precisely, refers to the anticipated fully sensual 'live-in' or 'englobing' environments that we will be able to enter by hooking ourselves up to a computer. Ideally, the computer will generate an illusion indistinguishable from the real thing. Primitive prototypes of virtual reality already exist.

virtual sex: see *cybersex.*

Notes

Introduction: The Road to Unreality

1. Constance L. Hays, 'Illusion and Tragedy Coexist After a Couple Dies,' *New York Times*, 7 January 1990.
2. I am aware, of course, that the term *reality*, problematic since Plato, has lately become a political minefield. So as not to be misunderstood, then, let me be as clear as possible. I have no problem with those who argue that reality, like taste, is subjective – a product of one's race, gender, economic class, education, and so on. These qualifications strike me as good and true. At the same time, however, I believe that under the strata of subjectivity, of language and perspective, lies a bedrock of fact: neo-Nazis in Koln or California may define the Holocaust differently than I do, yet the historical *fact* stands firm. It is *this* kind of reality – immutable, empirical, neither historically nor culturally relative – that I refer to here.
3. The rapid acceleration of cultural change in the twentieth century, of course, is a historical truism. One of the most vivid documents recording this transformation

in American culture (it originally appeared in 1929) is Robert S. and Helen M. Lynd, *Middletown: A Study in Contemporary American Culture* (New York: Harcourt Brace Jovanovich, 1959).

4. E. B. White, 'Removal,' reprinted in *One Man's Meat* (New York: Harper Colophon, 1983), 2-3.

5. Roger Cohen, 'Tito Lives Again But Like Ex-Nation, Is Bewildered,' *New York Times*, April 30, 1994, 4; Alma Guillermoprieto, 'Obsessed in Rio,' *The New Yorker* (August 16, 1993): 44-45. Guillermoprieto quotes a friend of hers as saying, 'Brazilians discovered virtual reality years ago. They never know when they are entering the [television] screen and when they are leaving it.'

6. Interview, Julian Dibbell, 'Net Prophet,' *Details* (August 1994): 100.

7. Ibid. 'It's eerie,' says Barlow's friend and editor of *Wired* magazine, Kevin Kelly, 'how much of life *can* be transferred. So far, some of the traits of the living that have successfully been transported to mechanical systems include self-replication, self-governance, limited self-repair, mild evolution, and partial learning.' Kevin Kelly, *Out of Control: The Rise of Neo-Biological Civilization* (Reading, Mass.: Addison-Wesley, 1994), 2. Kelly's science, as suggested by terms like 'mild evolution,' is suspect. More interesting, I think, is the sensibility behind the assertion.

8. Quarterman quoted in Peter H. Lewis, 'Cyberspace Is Looking a Lot Like Christmas,' *New York Times*, 25 December 1993. Timothy Ferris, 'The Future Is Coming,' *New York Times*, 12 November 1993.

9. Quoted in Andrew Pollack, 'Japanese Put a Human Face on Computers,' *New York Times*, 28 June 1994.

10. The term is from Allucquere Rosanne Stone, 'Will the

Real Body Please Stand Up?' in *Cyberspace: First Steps*, ed. Michael Benedikt (Cambridge, Mass.: MIT Press, 1991), 92.

11. Ibid., 94.
12. Langdon Winner, 'Do Artifacts Have Politics?' in *Technology and Politics*, ed. Michael E. Kraft and Norman J. Vig (Durham, N.C.: Duke University Press, 1988), 43.
13. Steve Lohr, 'For Computer Convention, Be Sure to Pack Vision,' *New York Times*, 24 September 1993.
14. There are notable exceptions, of course. Both Bill McKibben and Neil Postman, continuing in the honorable tradition of humanist/skeptics like Thomas Carlysle and H. G. Wells, have recently argued that technological advances have begun to separate us from the 'information' available only through direct, unmediated contact with the natural world (McKibben) and the values inherent in what we might broadly term humanistic culture (Postman). See Bill McKibben, *The Age of Missing Information* (New York: Random House, 1992), and Neil Postman, *Technopoly: The Surrender of Culture to Technology* (New York: Vintage Books, 1992).
15. The term is from the Intel Corporation's official videotape of Andrew S. Grove's keynote address at the PC Expo on 28 June 1994.
16. Kevin Kelly, 'Embrace It,' from 'The Electronic Hive: Two Views,' *Harper's Magazine* 288 (May 1994): 21. Kelly elaborates on his notion of the electronic hive in *Out of Control*, esp. pp. 11-28, and I elaborate on Kelly in chapter 4. Quote is from a letter by Robert Coover to *Harper's Magazine* 289 (August 1994): 4.
17. The estimate quoted here is from Steve Lohr, 'For Computer Convention, Be Sure to Pack Vision,' *New York Times*, 23 September 1993.

18. Quote is from a letter by John Perry Barlow to *Harper's Magazine* 289 (August 1994): 5.
19. Kevin Kelly, personal E-mail, 27 July 1994. The amusement park attitude is a common one among the digerati.
20. John Perry Barlow, personal E-mail, 22 July 1994.

Chapter 1: 'Reality Is Death'

1. Richard Kadrey, 'Pleasure by the Numbers,' *Future Sex* (premier issue, 1992): 7.
2. I am indebted here to Allucquere Rosanne Stone's excellent overview in 'Will the Real Body Please Stand Up?' in Michael Benedikt, ed., *Cyberspace: First Steps* (Cambridge, Mass.: MIT Press, 1991), 92-99.
3. I first heard this term used by Allucquere Rosanne Stone.
4. Michael Benedikt, 'Introduction,' in Benedikt, *Cyberspace*, 2.
5. Nicole Stenger, 'Mind Is a Leaking Rainbow,' in ibid., 56.
6. The 'safety' of cybersex, or tinysex, or teledildonics, is a selling point that links enthusiasts across the thoroughly blurred boundaries of high and low culture. For Richard Kadrey of *Future Sex*, 'VR sex . . . is the ultimate in safe sex: no HIV virus and no reason to be shy about trying out a new fetish.' For Paul Wu, president of Pixis International, which markets 'cyberporn' CD-ROMs, 'CD sex can even have its health benefits. With the prevalence of diseases,' he says, 'we're directing sexual energies. It's the ultimate

safe sex.' Wu quoted in Dean Takahashi, 'Sex Play in Cyberspace,' *Los Angeles Times*, 16 January 1994.

7. Michael Heim, 'The Erotic Ontology of Cyberspace,' in Benedikt, ed., *Cyberspace*, 61. Professor Heim is not alone in his vision. Julian Dibbell's slightly less buttoned-down (unbuttoned?) observations in *The Village Voice* make the same point: 'Amid flurries of even the most cursorily described caresses, sighs, and penetrations, the glands do engage, and often as throbbingly as they would in a real-life assignation . . . And if the virtual setting and the interplayer vibes are right, who knows? The heart may engage as well, stirring up passions as strong as many that bind lovers who observe *the formality* of trysting in the flesh' (my own, wondering italics). Julian Dibbell, 'Rape in Cyberspace: A Tale of Crime and Punishment on Line,' *The Village Voice*, 21 December 1993.

8. Stenger, 'Mind Is a Leaking Rainbow,' 51.

9. Benedikt, 'Introduction,' 14.

10. Stenger, 'Mind Is a Leaking Rainbow,' 53. The similarity between cyberspace theory and certain poststructuralist attitudes toward history, culture, and the self fashionable in academia reveals two things: (1) many if not most cyberspace theorists are academics; (2) poststructuralist attitudes toward the world are, at bottom, mechanistic (the current buzzword in the humanities and social sciences, for example, is *construction*), and therefore well suited to those interested in machines capable of breaking things down into their component parts.

11. Stone, 'Will the Real Body Please Stand Up?' 102. Indifference and sometimes downright hostility toward the natural world are underlying and often explicit themes in the literature of cyberspace – one of the stranger

responses, I believe, to the accelerating degradation of the environment in the second half of the twentieth century. I deal at some length with the environmental implications of the cyberspace revolution in chapter 3.

12. Stenger, 'Mind Is a Leaking Rainbow,' 56.
13. Benedikt, 'Introduction,' 10.
14. I am referring here to deconstruction – subsumed in its many incarnations under the rubric of post-structuralism – which has played such an enormous and influential role in American and European academic circles. Among the better critiques (there are many) of deconstructive criticism are Gerald Graff, *Literature Against Itself* (Chicago: University of Chicago Press, 1979).
15. Michiko Kakutani, 'When History and Memory Are Casualties: Holocaust Denial,' Critic's Notebook, *New York Times*, 30 April 1993. See also Kakutani, 'Opinion vs. Reality in an Age of Pundits,' Critic's Notebook, *New York Times*, 28 January 1994; Deborah E. Lipstadt, *Denying the Holocaust: The Growing Assault on Truth and Memory* (New York: Free Press, 1993); Robert Hughes, *Culture of Complaint: The Fraying of America* (New York: Oxford University Press, 1993); Gertrude Himmelfarb, *On Looking into the Abyss: Untimely Thoughts on Culture and Society* (New York: Knopf, 1994). On ethics and deconstruction, see David Lehman, *Signs of the Times: Deconstruction and the Fall of Paul De Man* (New York: Poseidon Press, 1991).
16. Part of the danger inherent in the deconstructionist argument – a danger inherent in any form of extremism – is that it will play into the hands of totalists on the other side. Absolutes, after all – concepts like 'natural law' and 'divine right' – *have* been used as tools of oppression throughout history. Revealing them for what they are,

therefore, is justified. Taken too far, though – and this is my point – relativism becomes an orthodoxy in its own right.

17. The fashionable nihilism I refer to is visible, for example, in Kevin Kelly, *Out of Control: The Rise of Neo-Biological Civilization* (Reading, Mass.: Addison-Wesley, 1994), in which the expression 'hip post-structuralist' appears frequently.

18. Stenger, 'Mind Is a Leaking Rainbow,' 53.

19. Brent Staples, for example, has argued eloquently that many of today's problems have low-tech solutions. Children, for example, increasingly dependent on television role models, require real individuals who will make a commitment to them in real life. Talking to them on the Internet won't help. See 'Role Models, Bogus and Real,' Editorial Notebook, *New York Times*, 24 June 1994.

Chapter 2: 'Springtime for Schizophrenia'

1. Quoted in Kevin Kelly, *Out of Control: The Rise of Neo-Biological Civilization* (Reading, Mass.: Addison-Wesley, 1994), 185.

2. KinkNet, FidoNet, and their like are special interest bulletin board networks usually linked together through the Internet.

3. The term is one of many lumping the nonwired into a single class of primitivists and Luddites.

4. Peter Rutten, Albert F. Bayers III, and Kelly Maloni, *Net Guide* (New York: Random House, 1994).

5. John Perry Barlow, 'Introduction,' in Rutten, Bayers, and Maloni, *Net Guide*, xvii.

6. Ibid., xix.
7. For a lively account of some of the problems, technical and otherwise, the newcomer to cyberspace can encounter, see Thomas E. Weber, 'Cyberspaced Out,' and Mary Lu Carnevale, 'World-Wide Web,' *Wall Street Journal*, 15 November 1993. 'For now,' notes Ms. Carnevale, expanding on the ever-elastic metaphor of the I-Way, 'the Internet remains an information highway with plenty of potholes, accidents and traffic jams.' The mechanical difficulties one encounters, of course, are compounded by the general attitude toward newcomers on the Net. Trolling for 'newbies' to 'flame' – looking for newcomers to insult – is a common pastime in cyberspace, and prizes have been established to reward those most adept at savaging unsuspecting neophytes. See Jared Sandberg's account in 'Up in Flames,' *Wall Street Journal*, 15 November 1993. While generally harmless – the average insults have all the wit of bathroom graffiti – this activity can make the Net less than user-friendly.
8. For a fascinating account of the world of Multiple User Dungeons, also referred to as Multiple User Dimensions, see David Bennahum, 'Fly Me to the MOO: Adventures in Textual Reality,' *Lingua Franca* (June 1994).
9. I am indebted here to Allucquere Rosanne Stone's overview of the world of 'consensual hallucinations' in 'Will the Real Body Please Stand Up?' in *Cyberspace: First Steps*, ed. Michael Benedikt (Cambridge, Mass.: MIT Press, 1991), 93-94.
10. Bennahum, 'Fly Me to the MOO,' 25.
11. Stone, 'Will the Real Body Please Stand Up?' 94.
12. Julian Dibbell, 'Rape in Cyberspace: A Tale of Crime

and Punishment On-Line,' *The Village Voice*, 21 December 1993.

13. The potential real-world implications of virtual criminal behavior are a legal nightmare waiting to begin. Allucquere Rosanne Stone notes that one of the issues currently being debated by futurist attorneys is what liability an individual would have were his behavior in VR to cause his victim a real-world heart attack. Other, perhaps more immediate concerns surround the issues of character defamation and privacy. See Stone, 'Will the Real Body Please Stand Up?' 84.

14. The latest on-line rumors surrounding the Bungle case had victims locating the E-mail address of the individual behind the Bungle persona and exposing his behavior to his real-world employer. I have no way of affirming this, of course.

15. See Philip Elmer-Dewitt, 'The Amazing Video Game Boom,' *Time*, 27 September 1993, 70-72.

16. Dibbell himself admits the disorienting power of the cyberspace community and its surreal residents, noting: 'I fear I may have shape-shifted by the digital moonlight one too many times' for full objectivity. Dibbell, 'Rape in Cyberspace,' 37.

17. Bennahum, 'Fly Me to the MOO,' 26.

18. A 1963 painting by the Belgian surrealist René Magritte is the best visual rendering of the spirit of cyberspace I know. The painting, 'The Field Glass,' shows a large double-paned window set into a dark, interior wall. Through the glass panes we can see a benign summer sky with fluffy cumulus clouds – a reassuring, even banal play on the Romantic concept of the painting as a window onto the world. The kicker lies in the fact that the window is slightly open. Visible through the narrow space between the panes is a black void. Making

the image even more unsettling, a bit of the interior window frame shows through a corner of the glass. Instead of a window onto the world, we are offered a landscape suggesting that all reality is potentially illusion.

19. One of the most common experiences among people who enter cyberspace communities – and eloquent proof of how enveloping the medium can be – is the distortion of time in the real world. 'If I didn't have to eat, sleep, or pee,' one resident told me, 'I'd never come out.'

20. Dibbell, 'Rape in Cyberspace,' 38.

21. John Seabrook, 'My First Flame,' *The New Yorker*, 6 June 1994.

22. The analogy, a common one in cyberspace, is borne out by the terminology of virtual reality; electronic fantasy worlds are regularly referred to as MUSHes: *M*ultiple *U*ser *S*hared *H*allucination.

23. In 'Will the Real Body Please Stand Up?' (102-5) Allucquere Rosanne Stone discusses the relationship between cybersex and phone sex, and concludes that 'fortunately or unfortunately . . . everyone is still preorgasmic in virtual reality.' Not so in cyberspace, where, as David Bennahum points out, specialty MOOs like FurryMuck, on which half-human, half-animal creatures come together to have Netsex, make for a great deal of 'rapid one-handed typing.' Of course, since sitting alone at a terminal can be a social act, so can masturbation.

24. Ibid., 99-105.

25. Nicole Stenger, 'Mind Is a Leaking Rainbow,' in Benedikt, *Cyberspace*, 53.

26. Dibbell, 'Rape in Cyberspace,' 38.

27. Stone, 'Will the Real Body Please Stand Up?' 85.

Chapter 3: Virtual World

1. Quoted in Kevin Kelly, *Out of Control: The Rise of Neo-Biological Civilization* (Reading, Mass.: Addison-Wesley, 1994), 171.
2. Wendy A. Kellogg, John M. Carroll, and John T. Richards, 'Making Reality a Cyberspace,' in *Cyberspace: First Steps*, ed. Michael Benedikt (Cambridge, Mass.: MIT Press, 1991), 412-13. The authors note, however, that the enclosed virtual world will still have its place. In the museum of the future, for example, 'visitors might enter enclosed habitat cyberspaces in which they can experience an animal's environment by becoming the animal virtually.'
3. Gregory Stock, *Metaman: The Merging of Humans and Machines into a Global Superorganism* (New York: Simon and Schuster, 1993), 182. Hensen quoted in Kelly, *Out of Control*, 49. Karakotsios quoted in ibid., 349-50.
4. Kellogg, Carroll, and Richards, 'Making Reality a Cyberspace,' 412-13.
5. Allucquere Rosanne Stone, 'Will the Real Body Please Stand Up?' in Benedikt, *Cyberspace*, 102.
6. Kelly, *Out of Control*, 350.
7. For more on developments in the field of artificial life, see Steven Levy, *Artificial Life: The Quest for a New Creation* (New York: Pantheon, 1992). On the Human Genome Project and other genetic research, see Robert Cook-Deegan, *The Gene Wars* (New York: Norton, 1993), as well as John Seabrook's excellent review, 'Building a Better Human,' in *The New Yorker* (28 March 1994). Seabrook's review raises the issue of ethics that Cook-Deegan, and many others, seem uninterested in. For Seabrook, as for myself, the essential question is not Can we? but Should we?

8. Bruce Mazlish, *The Fourth Discontinuity: The Co-Evolution of Humans and Machines* (New Haven: Yale University Press, 1993), 8.

9. A certain whackiness, to put it indelicately, seems at times an occupational hazard among technoevangelists. See, for example, Gregory Stock's examples of 'mimicry and camouflage' in the machine realm in *Metaman*, 62-63.

10. See Steward Brand, *The Media Lab: Inventing the Future at MIT* (New York: Viking, 1987), 8. Brand describes the relationship between MIT and its many suitors at some length. In brief, in exchange for funding – lots of it – the 'outside interests' get 'products' developed by the university. The new products, in turn, bring a profit for the university (MIT currently holds the world record – 19 million dollars – for royalties from a single technology), as well as more funding. The only thing missing from the feedback loop is the issue of ethics.

11. Ibid., 54-55. The dream of 'sensitive' or 'personalized' technology, of course, is central to much that goes on at the Media Lab, and therefore a running theme throughout Brand's book. Many of the products first envisioned in places like the Media Lab – from personalized newspapers to phones that take voice commands – are already entering the market. Others, like intelligent computer agents – micro-organisms that can make their way through the nation's computer networks and do their owner's bidding – are about to make their entrance. See John Markoff, 'Hopes and Fears on New Computer Organisms,' *New York Times*, 6 January 1994. For a fascinating overview of what's on the horizon, see James Gleick, 'The Telephone Transformed – into Almost Everything,' *New York Times Magazine*, 16 May 1993.

12. The imminence of the techno-millennium is a given among the technoevangelists, as it is among more strictly religious millennialists.

13. Brand, *The Media Lab*, 116; Mazlish, *The Fourth Discontinuity*, 184.

14. Mazlish, *The Fourth Discontinuity*, 182, 218-19.

15. Brand, *The Media Lab*, 9.

16. Andrew Pollack, 'To Surf and Ski, the Japanese Are Heading Indoors,' *New York Times*, 15 June 1993.

17. Comments on sex scene techniques are by Paul Wu, president of Pixis Interactive, quoted in Dean Takahashi, 'Sex Play in Cyberspace,' *Los Angeles Times*, 16 January 1994. See also John Tierney's excellent overview of the relation between technology and pornography in 'Porn, the Low-Slung Engine of Progress,' *New York Times*, 9 January 1994.

18. Quoted in Stephanie Strom, 'Testing the High Hopes for TV Shopping,' *New York Times*, 3 January 1994.

19. The introduction of the word *virtual* into the national lexicon implies an inversion of values strikingly similar, in some ways, to the inversion associated with the introduction of the word *spiritual* at the dawn of Christianity. By adding the adjective *spiritual* to life and death, Christianity inverted those words' earlier meaning. Life and death, in other words, were no longer understood primarily in terms of the body, but rather the spirit. Under this new calculus, physical life came to be understood as spiritual death, and physical death, as spiritual life. With the digital revolution, the transforming adjective is *virtual*.

20. Quoted in Kelly, *Out of Control*, 314.

21. Stock, *Metaman*, 204.

22. Their perspective on the works they quote, as one might expect, tends to be both highly idiosyncratic and

tinged with a certain lack of humility. Bruce Mazlish, for example, finds Karel Capek's classic play *R.U.R.* an 'incredibly muddled,' 'ultimately baffling,' 'poorly written hodgepodge of mostly improbable ideas' (a striking illustration of the danger of throwing stones from glass houses), and its author both 'disingenuous' and stupid. Kevin Kelly, in turn, dispenses with George Orwell, offering in his place one Jay David Bolter. 'The ever insightful Bolter,' Kelly notes, has shown conclusively that computers are about 'heterogeneity, individualization, and autonomy.' Needless to say, Orwell's predictions, on the whole, remain both uncannily prescient and altogether accurate.

23. E. M. Forster, 'The Machine Stops,' *Modern Short Stories* (New York: Oxford University Press, 1951).

24. Kelly, *Out of Control*, 440. John Holusha, 'AT&T Proposes Sea Cable That Would Encircle Africa,' *New York Times*, 26 April 1994.

25. At a recent art auction, one of Bill Gates's representatives, charged with buying up the electronic rights to various art works, was asked if his boss knew the differences between an original work of art and a reproduction. 'He certainly does,' was the answer, 'and he much prefers the reproduction.' Neil Morgan, 'Bill Gates Would Prefer Electronic Van Gogh,' *San Diego Union-Tribune*, 9 June 1994.

Chapter 4: Highway to Hive

1. A prime example from the mid-range is Michael J. O'Neill, *The Roar of the Crowd: How Television and People*

Power Are Changing the World (New York: Times Books, 1993). The fringe is well represented by Kevin Kelly, *Out of Control: The Rise of Neo-Biological Civilization* (Reading, Mass.: Addison-Wesley, 1994).

2. John Markoff, 'The Lost Art of Getting Lost,' *New York Times*, 18 September 1994.

3. Peter H. Lewis, 'Preaching the Techno-Gospel, Al Gore Version,' *New York Times*, 17 January 1994.

4. The association is not entirely specious. Bruce Dern and his robotic friend, we recall, willingly cast themselves off to save the last surviving rain forest, which had been slated for destruction. The vice president, as we know, also has an eco-angle; lest we forget, the image of the Earth that frames Mr. Gore in cyberspace is there to remind us. It is the same image that appears on the cover of his book, *Earth in the Balance* (Boston: Houghton-Mifflin, 1992). In short, the photographic image of the Earth works as a sort of visual ligature, connecting environmentalism to cyberspace, books to binary code, the earlier, plaid-shirted, environmental vice president to the newly reconstituted vice president of the Infobahn. They are all compatible, we are being told. There are no contradictions.

5. Noted in 'Harper's Index,' *Harper's Magazine* (April 1994).

6. The terms *conversion* and *communion* appear regularly throughout the technoevangelists' works, for example, in Howard Rheingold's *The Virtual Community: Homesteading on the Electronic Frontier* (Reading, Mass.: Addison-Wesley, 1993). 'Blessed are the poor' quote is from Anthony Ramirez, 'Providing for the Have-Nots of the New Information Age,' Ideas and Trends, *New York Times*, 23 January 1994.

7. Nathaniel C. Nash, 'Gore Sees World Data Privatization,' *New York Times*, 22 March 1994.

8. Scholars like Ellen Hume, a senior fellow at the Annenberg Washington Program on Communications Policy, have wondered the same thing. Even more revealing, perhaps, is the fact that the digerati themselves have noticed the gap between rhetoric and Net reality. In his interview with John Perry Barlow, Julian Dibbell asks: 'Have you noticed a certain ironic chasm between your sweeping visions of where cyberspace is headed and the fact that so much of the discussion coursing through the Net is the most banal chitchat?' Barlow: 'Yeah. (laughs) It's CB radio, only typing.' See Julian Dibbell, 'Net Prophet,' *Details* (August 1994).

9. Though democracy may not follow fiber-optic cable, consumerism certainly will. What this suggests, as Matthew Connelly and Paul Kennedy recently noted, is that the world communication revolution will enable the industrialized West to beam images of plenty to all those struggling to attain a sufficient daily intake of calories. Rather than making the world more integrated (or uniformly well-off), it will succeed only in making the world more envious. See Connelly and Kennedy, 'Must It Be the Rest Against the West?' *Atlantic Monthly* (December 1994).

10. The tradition of technological utopianism has been an American tradition for nearly two centuries. See Leo Marx's classic *The Machine in the Garden: Technology and the Pastoral Ideal in America* (London: Oxford University Press, 1964), and Howard P. Segal, *Technological Utopianism in American Culture* (Chicago: University of Chicago Press, 1985).

11. Some of the darker implications of the frontier analogy are discussed by Lewis Lapham, 'Robber Barons Redux,' *Harper's Magazine* (January 1994).

Lapham's extension of the cyberspace/frontier metaphor goes something like this. The huge communications conglomerates – John C. Mallone's TCI, for example – are carving up the free territory in an orgy of deregulation loosed by the hapless Clinton administration. They are setting up tollbooths, privatizing access ramps, even monopolizing the information roadways themselves, all in 'the spirit of implacable and well-organized greed.' In their power, their ruthlessness, their often explicit contempt for antitrust laws, they are indistinguishable from the infamous monopolies of the Gilded Age; the men who run them, by extension, are the latter-day equals of Vanderbilt, Morgan, and John D. Rockefeller.

12. Lately, a new generation of frontiersmen has begun to combine the escapist fantasies of the Net with something resembling real life, lighting out (or talking about lighting out) for Montana or Alaska, leaving behind an electronic trail of bread crumbs connecting them to friends, family, and job. As a parody of the American traditions of individualism and self-reliance, this sort of Have-Mac-Will-Travel sensibility should be funny. The reason it's not, particularly, is because what *seems* like self-sufficiency is actually its precise opposite. As the new frontiersman sits by his computer station in the wilderness, cherishing his freedom from shaving, he is actually reaffirming his utter dependence on the new information technologies and the powers behind them.

13. Sacvan Bercovitch, professor of American literature at Harvard University, has demonstrated the phenomenal adaptability of the millennial myth of America, which has endured, as both a rhetorical form and a ritual of socialization, from John Winthrop to Ronald Reagan.

The millennial cast of the digital revolution is the myth's latest incarnation: to realize the promise of America today – to reach the New Canaan at last – we must ascend into cyberspace with John Perry Barlow. See Sacvan Bercovitch, *The American Jeremiad* (Madison: University of Wisconsin Press, 1978).

14. The homogeneity to which I refer is hidden behind the apparent diversity of the communication revolution, which, while offering us infinitely personalized technologies and the 'individualism' implicit in five hundred television channels, is actually just cementing us in a deeper sameness – the sameness of the consumer (of information and products) with a million (largely irrelevant) choices. Neil Postman puts it well: 'We propose to spend billions on a super-information network. To do what? Instead of 60 TV channels, we'll have 500, maybe a thousand. We'll have access to more entertainment, more sports, more commercials, more news – faster, more conveniently, in more diverse forms. We will, in other words, flood our lives with that from which we are already drowning.' See 'We Are the Wired: Some Views on the Fiberoptic Ties That Bind,' *New York Times*, 24 October 1993.

15. For a marvelous account of the cultural price incurred in our move from the back road to the interstate, see William Least Heat Moon, *Blue Highways: A Journey into America* (New York: Ballantine, 1982).

16. Gregory Stock, *Metaman: The Merging of Humans and Machines into a Global Superorganism* (New York: Simon and Schuster, 1993), 137.

17. Kevin Kelly, 'Embrace It,' in 'The Electronic Hive: Two Views,' *Harper's Magazine* (May 1994).

18. Kelly, *Out of Control*, 28.

19. 'Apparent individuals' quote in ibid., 102. Minsky

quoted at length in ibid., 43-44. '*Beyond* Homo sapiens' is the title of chapter 9 in Stock, *Metaman*.

20. Stock, *Metaman*, 119, 135.
21. Ibid., 211.
22. Ibid., 209.
23. Kelly, *Out of Control*, 102-3.
24. Stock, *Metaman*, 20. We're also 'evolving' away from nature, according to Stock. 'No longer,' he points out, 'do we relate to "nature" as our actual living environment.' Few, he adds, 'will long endure – much less enjoy – slogging through a fetid swamp, shivering in a cold penetrating wind, or standing in a swarm of mosquitos. And why should we?' Humanity, he sums up, is moving inside, into the synthetic, managed environment. The massive extinction of species, therefore, is a nonissue. They will be replaced by technobiological hybrids. See *Metaman*, 186.
25. Kelly, *Out of Control*, 440.
26. Stock, *Metaman*, 79.
27. Quoted in Kelly, *Out of Control*, 452.
28. Ibid., 233.
29. In view of the lack of scrutiny the technoevangelists enjoy – despite the massive amounts of federal funding flowing into places like MIT's Media Lab – damping down the god talk makes sense. 'Nobody political has paid the slightest bit of attention to Negroponte or the Media Lab,' writes Steward Brand in *The Media Lab: Inventing the Future at MIT* (New York: Viking, 1987), 8. That might change, of course, were the technoevangelists' sermons to begin reaching a wider audience.
30. Kelly, 'Embrace It,' 21.
31. If the parallel sounds alarmist, I do not apologize. Homogeneity, as George Kennan and many others

have pointed out over the years, has always been a primary, and perhaps an indispensable, ingredient to totalitarianism, and today we're in the process of embracing a new technology that asks us to sacrifice our individual selves to an abstraction, a technology whose proponents no longer even pretend that the loss of individualism is something to be avoided.

Chapter 5: A Republic of Illusion

1. Ada Louise Huxtable, 'Inventing American Reality,' *New York Review of Books*, 3 December 1992.
2. Quoted in John Tierney, 'Jung in Motion, Virtually, and Other Computer Fuzz,' *New York Times*, 16 September 1993.
3. Umberto Eco, *Travels in Hyperreality* (New York: Harcourt Brace Jovanovich, 1986).
4. Michael Kelly, 'David Gergen, Master of the Game,' *New York Times Magazine*, 31 October 1993.
5. That momentum, of course, makes virtually *any* assessment of the status quo difficult – including this one.
6. I realize, of course, that cultural conversations are also about power; the distinction I draw, therefore – a largely subjective one – is one of form and degree. Cultural conversations, as I see them, are less explicit, less overt in their desire for power, less quick to translate their victories into real-world gain.
7. See Huxtable, 'Inventing American Reality,' for an extended discussion of the virtual reality of theme parks in general, and Colonial Williamsburg in particular.
8. Kim Eastham, 'Artifishal Experience,' *Wired* (July 1994): 122.

9. Quoted in ibid.
10. Kim Eastham, 'The Virtual Brat,' *Wired* (August 1994): 104.
11. Quoted in ibid.
12. Stewart Brand, for example, discusses at length the progress made in places like MIT's Media Lab to simulate physical sensation electronically. '"Force feedback,"' he points out, already 'permits computer simulation of almost any physical interaction.' See Brand, *The Media Lab: Inventing the Future at MIT* (New York: Viking, 1987), unnumbered caption for illustration on fourteenth page of unnumbered illustration section; also 146-48.
13. Quoted in Eastham, 'The Virtual Brat,' 104.
14. The analogy drawn between the marketing of Doom and addictive drugs is from Peter H. Lewis, 'Virtual Mayhem and Real Profits,' *New York Times*, 3 September 1994. Lewis notes that 'by using a marketing strategy they acknowledge is similar to the way drugs are dealt – give away the first episode, then sell subsequent episodes once the customer is hooked – the young owners of Id Software Inc. [have] built a fast-growing company.'
15. Quoted in Joel Bleifuss, 'New Angles from the Spin Doctors,' Viewpoints, *New York Times*, 20 March 1994.
16. William J. Mitchell, 'When Is Seeing Believing?' *Scientific American* (February 1994): 73.
17. The gesture, of course, is as desperate as it is hopeless. One might as well expect the population at large to resist a technology capable of printing utterly undetectable twenty-dollar bills. Many will; some, alas, will not. In light of all this, one must give serious consideration to the digerati claim that the age of photography – as a representational medium with any claim on 'reality' –

is over. See Steward Brand's fascinating discussion in *The Media Lab*, 219-23.

18. Quoted in William Glaberson, 'Newsday Imagines an Event, and Sets Off a Debate,' *New York Times*, 17 February 1994.

19. Michael Benedikt, ed., *Cyberspace: First Steps* (Cambridge, Mass.: MIT Press, 1991), 10.

20. Irwin S. Kirsch, Ann Jungeblut, Lynn Jenkins, and Andrew Kolstad, *Adult Literacy in America: A First Look at the Results of the National Adult Literacy Survey* (Educational Testing Service, 1993), xiv-xv.

21. Quoted in Aljean Harmetz, 'Two Special Effects (a Crib Sheet),' *New York Times*, 24 July 1994.

22. Daniel Boorstin, *The Image: A Guide to Pseudo-Events in America* (New York: Harper-Colophon, 1961), 183. Boorstin's book, published long before the popularization of computer technologies, is still the pioneering work on virtual reality in the broader, cultural sense, and an invaluable aid in assessing how far the tyranny of the image has progressed over the second half of this century.

23. Kevin Kelly, *Out of Control: The Rise of Neo-Biological Civilization (Reading, Mass.*: Addison-Wesley, 1994), 240.

24. Quote from Glaberson, 'Newsday Imagines.'

25. The technical ability to rearrange visual historical records may well usher in a new era of propaganda, but it is important to note that on the rhetorical level, this kind of manipulation of historical reality has been a staple of politics for some time, though perhaps not to the extent seen today. Though the Reagan administration was arguably the first to treat foreign policy as a subset of virtual reality, later administrations have not been immune. See, for example, Douglas Jehl, 'Officials Told

to Avoid Calling Rwanda Killings "Genocide,"' *New York Times*, 10 June 1994.

26. Quoted in Michael Wines, 'Disney Will Recreate U.S. History Next to a Place Where It Was Made,'*New York Times*, 12 November 1993.

27. See Huxtable, 'Inventing American Reality.'

Chapter 6: The Case for Essentialism

1. Whether the digital revolution is good business in the long run remains highly questionable. In addition to the threat posed by advertising on the Internet to *actual* stores, and the productivity wasted on high-tech gadgetry and office computer games, there is the issue of thousands being laid off – by IBM and AT&T, for example – because their companies are migrating into cyberspace. 'Cyberspace,' says Richard Sclove, the executive director of the Loka Institute, a public policy research center in Amherst, Massachusetts, 'is going to finish what Walmart started.' See John Markoff, 'Staking a Claim on the Virtual Frontier,' *New York Times*, 2 January 1994. For more on both the financial and human costs of the digital revolution, see Kirk Johnson, 'Hi-Tech Mobile Workers Transform the Face and Culture of Companies,' *New York Times*, 8 February 1994.

2. My argument here is shared by Virginia Abernathy, 'Optimism and Overpopulation,' *Atlantic Monthly* (December 1994): 91.

3. Walter B. Wriston, *The Twilight of Sovereignty: How the Information Revolution Is Transforming Our World* (New York: Scribner's, 1992); Robert Reich, *The Work of*

Nations: Preparing Ourselves for 21st-Century Capitalism
(Knopf, 1991). For both Wriston and Reich, the information revolution is all about increasing market share,
anticipating the collapse of borders, and controlling the
great winds of capital that already circumnavigate the
globe at the touch of a button. Howard Rheingold,
*The Virtual Community: Homesteading on the Electronic
Frontier* (New York: Harper Perennial, 1993).

4. It's striking – and disheartening – to note that many
of today's technoevangelists are actually apostate environmentalists and self-described 1960s counterculture
types who, apparently having found the real world and
its problems too discouraging, decided to seek Eden
elsewhere.

5. E. O. Wilson, 'Biophilia and the Conservation Ethic,'
in *The Biophilia Hypothesis*, ed. Stephen R. Kellert and
Edward O. Wilson (Washington: Island Press, 1993),
32; Robert L. Park, 'Genetics and the I of the Universe,'
op-ed, *New York Times*, 16 August 1993.

6. The key issue here is the speed of technological
progress. All technologies, one could argue, from
the first primitive skin scrapers of the Neolithic,
have limited the domain of the real – that was
their purpose, and it remains their purpose today.
What's striking, though, is that the development of
tools, which for two and a half million years was
so gradual as to be invisible to the human eye, has
within the space of our lifetimes gathered tremendous
velocity. In fact, this acceleration seems to have been
building throughout human history; each successive
technological age has been of shorter duration than
the one before it. All of which suggests two problems:
(1) the pace of change has outstripped our ability to
adapt; and (2) as our technologies have grown better

at subjugating the real world, they've finally arrived at the point at which they can replace it altogether.

7. Winifred Gallagher, *The Power of Place: How Our Surroundings Shape Our Thoughts, Emotions, and Actions* (New York: Poseidon Press, 1993); Orr quote from William K. Stevens, 'Want a Room with a View? Idea May Be in the Genes,' *New York Times*, 20 October 1993.

8. Anne Raver, 'Patients Discover the Power of Gardens,' *New York Times*, 29 December 1994.

9. Daniel Goleman, 'Stress and Isolation Tied to a Reduced Life Span,' *New York Times*, 7 May 1993; Lauren K. Ayers, 'Cancer Activists Boost Immune Response,' letter to the editor, *New York Times*, 11 November 1994.

10. Brent Staples, 'Life in the Information Age: When Burma-Shave Meets Cyberspace,' Editorial Notebook, *New York Times*, 7 July 1994.

11. See Peter H. Lewis, 'In Cyberspace, a High-tech League of Their Own,' *New York Times*, 5 April 1994.

12. Brent Staples, 'The End of Solitude: Thoreau Says "No" to Beeper Bondage,' Editorial Notebook, *New York Times*, 14 June 1994.

13. Quoted in James Gleick, 'The Telephone Transformed – into Almost Everything,' *New York Times Magazine*, 16 May 1993.

14. Neil Postman, *Technopoly: The Surrender of Culture to Technology* (New York: Vintage, 1993), 60.

15. Quoted in 'The Great Escape from Silicon Valley,' in 'The Executive Life,' *New York Times*, 27 February 1994; Timothy Egan, 'It Takes Time to Build a Xanadu for Citizen Gates,' *New York Times*, 12 January 1995.

16. George Gilder, *Life After Television: The Coming Transformation of Media and American Life* (New York: Norton, 1992).

17. James Barron, 'A New Species of Couch Potato Takes Root,' *New York Times*, 16 November 1994.

18. Quoted in ibid.

19. Minow's 'vast wasteland' characterization is from his famous 1961 speech, given while serving as chairman of the Federal Communications Commission.

20. Quoted in Bryan Miller, 'No Spare Moments in the High-Tech Life,' *New York Times*, 25 April 1994. As Miller amply demonstrates, a backlash to the over-stimulation brought about by the communications revolution is appearing across the cultural spectrum.

21. See John Markoff, 'Interactive Video Setup for Children,' Company News, *New York Times*, 29 March 1994. The odd notion of children 'socializing' in cyberspace is an advertising staple. In fact, recent ads go so far as to claim that computer programs will specifically *teach* a child social skills.

22. Quoted in ibid. Denise Caruso has been one of the more reasonable and balanced voices in the computer industry, often acting as a kind of rational counterweight to the technoevangelists' more outrageous predictions. See, for example, Denise Caruso, 'Ahead of Ourselves,' *Wall Street Journal*, 15 November 1993.

23. Of course, how knowledge, for example, is interpreted is another thing. One of the concepts currently making the rounds is 'visual literacy,' which until recently used to be known as 'illiteracy.'

24. Nicole Stenger, 'Mind Is a Leaking Rainbow,' in *Cyberspace: First Steps*, ed. Michael Benedikt (Cambridge, Mass.: MIT Press, 1991), 57.

25. The pugnacity of the digerati is worth noting. In a recent interview in *Wired* magazine, for example, John Malone, veteran of the telecommunications wars and head of TCI, suggested that the best way to get the

information highway running by the end of 1996 might be for someone to shoot the head of the FCC. When offered the opportunity to explain that he was joking, Malone declined. In short, the true evangelists are not an easygoing bunch; their willingness to savage, ridicule, and/or demonize nondevotees is one of their more notable characteristics. See David Kline, 'Infobahn Warrior,' *Wired* (July 1994).

26. The obvious issue here – it's a point that bears repeating – is profit. The lending library, the playground, the individual imagination, the conversation we can have with a neighbor – all these things are free and available to everyone. Computers cost money.

27. See Walter Benjamin, *Illuminations* (New York: Schocken Books, 1969). Benjamin's classic essay 'The Work of Art in the Age of Mechanical Reproduction' argues, in part, that mechanical reproduction has destroyed the 'aura' of the original work of art. In our virtual age, of course, Benjamin's essay asks a very important question: Can reality, like the work of art, be robbed of its aura? I believe it can, and has been, to a great extent, already.

28. See Sven Birkerts, 'Refuse It,' in 'The Electronic Hive: Two Views,' *Harper's Magazine* (May 1994). Birkerts's eloquent essay is adapted from his forthcoming book, *The Gutenberg Elegies: The Fate of Reading in an Electronic Age* (New York: Faber and Faber, 1994), which, to my regret, came out too late for me to consult.

29. For an overview of some of the voices of caution from within academia, see Colleen Cordes, 'Technology as Religion?' *Chronicle of Higher Education*, 27 April 1994.

30. Vaclav Havel has made the same point, more eloquently, throughout his career; the importance of dedicating ourselves to the pursuit of truth runs

like a leitmotif through his life and his work. His qualifications regarding 'universalist solutions,' for that reason, are particularly worth quoting: 'Man's attitude to the world,' he notes, 'must be radically changed. We have to abandon the arrogant belief that the world is merely a puzzle to be solved, a machine with instructions for use waiting to be discovered, a body of information to be fed into a computer in the hope that, sooner or later, it will spit out a universalist solution.' Vaclav Havel, address to the World Economic Forum, Davos, Switzerland, 4 February 1992, excerpted in 'The End of the Modern Era,' op-ed, *New York Times*, 1 March 1992.

31. Joseph Wood Krutch, *The Twelve Seasons: A Perpetual Calendar for the Country* (New York: William Sloane, 1949), 11.

32. One of the most powerful and humane arguments for reintegrating nature and culture is Donald Worster's *The Wealth of Nature: Environmental History and the Ecological Imagination* (Oxford: Oxford University Press, 1993). For an overview of some of the figures within the academic community asking the hard questions regarding technological progress, see Cordes, 'Technology as Religion?'

33. E. B. White, 'Removal,' reprinted in *One Man's Meat* (New York: Harper Colophon, 1983), 3.